LOSS&LEGACY

LOSS  LEGACY

The Half-Century Quest To Reclaim
A Birthright Stolen By The Nazis

Sam A. Gronner

Full Court Press
Englewood Cliffs, New Jersey

Second Printing

Copyright © 2020 by AMTA Legacy Partners, LLC

Published in the United States of America
by Full Court Press, 601 Palisade Avenue,
Englewood Cliffs, NJ 07632
fullcourtpress.com

ISBN 978-1-946989-49-9
Library of Congress Control Number: 2020903194

Editing and book design by Barry Sheinkopf

Cover design by Barry Sheinkopf and Bob Eichinger

Author photo by Barbara Balkin

FOR THE GRANDCHILDREN
Arielle, Jesse, Matt, and Ben

AND THE FOURTH GENERATION,
Maia, Liora, and Jacob

Acknowledgments

From the outset, I had resolved that my memoir would not be an encyclopedic family history. Nor would it be a genealogical research project replete with documentary evidence like birth certificates, death records and photos of headstones.

I am neither a historian nor a professional genealogist, and I make no pretense of being an expert on these topics. Handicapped by not having witnessed some of the events I recount, I resisted spinning a fictional tale, with detailed and vivid accounts of the actors central to the story—especially those whom I had never known.

Instead, I approached the subject from my journalistic comfort zone. This account describes my own eyewitness experience with a parent who was relentless in pursuing a stolen past. My reporting relies on what I personally remember or discovered in research, and on documents provided by, or stories I had heard from, relatives, friends and trusted sources.

When I initially met him to discuss the Leo Baeck Institute's potential interest in a book about my family, Frank Mecklenburg encouraged me to dive into my family roots in Silesia, the birthplace of my grandfather. One would expect this counsel from LBI's chief archivist. But despite my reluctance to step too deeply into the quicksand of genealogical research, his prompting did lead me to a research trip to Cieszyn, Poland. Thankfully I discovered Jacek Proszyk, Ph.D., one of the foremost scholars on the former Jewish community, who located the documentation on my grandfather's childhood.

The earliest part of my family lore is based on the work of two collaborators I mention in the narrative. Yoram Grinspan, my second cousin in Israel, has reconstructed an expansive family tree that opened the window to our common familial relationships linked to our respective Sandler-surnamed grandmothers—Helene, my father's mother, and her sister Paula. Yoram was the source of the revealing letters my grandparents sent to relatives who resettled in pre-state Israel. My second cousin Peter Weil of Chicago, grandson of Wilhelm, another sibling of my grandmother, has published his own memoir of the Weil-Sandler family. I am grateful to Yoram and Peter for their diligent review of my manuscript.

The history of the small Jewish community in Ilmenau, including the fate of the families who fell victim to the Nazi regime, has been documented since the reunification of Germany in 1989. I relied on previous narratives by Gerlinde Hoefert and acknowledge the help provided by Martina Arnold, the city archivist, who transcribed documents handwritten by my grandfather. I am grateful to Juliane Rauprich, Ph.D., for the friendship and support she lent by sharing archival information dug up from official Gestapo files. I appreciate the time that Heinz Geitz, prominent attorney in Ilmenau, devoted to review the manuscript section describing his success in restoring my father's stolen inheritance.

Above all, my greatest admiration and gratitude is directed at Rainer Borsdorf. He tirelessly continues to search, and collect evidence and anecdotes about, Ilmenau's former Jewish neighbors, at times making use of relevant vintage photographs from the collection of his collaborator Berndt Frankenberger. I look forward to assist and promote Rainer's personal commitment to remembrance, coupled with his advocacy of democratic ideals.

I am blessed with friendships that evolved from the bonds of our parents' generation, and grateful to have my fading memory of childhood refreshed by friends like Roni Benjamin, Aliza Erber, and Gabi Barziv.

My sister Tammy Kallman and I are committed to perpetuate the lessons drawn from our father's life. She and I are united in our mission to immediately confront words of hate or bigotry directed at any group of people.

I thank my daughter, Arielle Gronner, and my niece, Kate McGuire, for the time and attention they dedicated to reviewing the manuscript to improve clarity, and narrative style. Special thanks go to Barry Sheinkopf, my editor and publisher, for his keen eyes and sharp blue pencil, ushering my manuscript into a compelling final product.

Although my parents are now gone, I cannot escape the fact that their story would have faded into oblivion, and the associated documents and photos relegated to the waste basket, had not my son Jesse asked me to visit his grandfather's birthplace, and had not Karen, my life partner, been insistent that I clear out the carton of memorabilia in our bedroom closet. It is because of them that this book exists.

—S.A.G.

Author's Note

"I begin with the young. We older ones are used up. We are rotten to the marrow. But my magnificent youngsters! Are there any finer ones in the world? What material! With them I can make a new world."

--Adolf Hitler, ca. 1933

As children of Holocaust survivors, we members of the Second Generation are obliged to promptly sound an alarm at the first expression of hate toward any group on account of their faith, ethnicity, race, national origin or gender identity. Our father left us an indelible truth: Mere words laid the groundwork for what was to become the most heinous example of mankind's inhumanity.

Contemporary students are just as vulnerable to propaganda as in Hitler's time, but today it is being spread on digital and social media platforms. Hence, it's imperative that I extend the reach of this work into the digital domain, beginning with an e-book version funded by sales of this book. I also want to support programs that enable students to discern what is propaganda in this digital-centered age.

Lastly, for digital preservation, I am donating my source materials to the Leo Baeck Institute, the world's premier archive of the history and culture of German Jewry.

Table of Contents

Preface

The whitewashed *Theodor Herzl*, the new passenger liner that Zim Lines had acquired earlier in the year, stood out against the Mediterranean while docked at the harbor in Haifa. Once we boarded, glancing to the east from the ship's upper deck, bright sunlight rising from behind Mount Carmel gleamed off the prominent golden dome of the Bahá'í Temple.

It was September 1957, just days shy of my tenth birthday. I stood aft on the ocean liner's open deck, capturing the receding vista of Haifa and the harbor, as we embarked on what my parents had told me was a brief visit to my uncle and aunt in France, the first time I would meet "Onkel Rudy" and "Tante Lydie." (As with many families with German-speaking roots, referred to as Jeckes, older relatives were referred to by their German titles, such as "Opa" and "Oma" for my maternal grandparents. Acquiescing to the official status of Hebrew in the new State of Israel, Jecke children like my sister, our Israeli cousin and I all called our parents "Aba" for Dad and "Ima" for Mom.)

Until then, I had only met the first cousins on my mother's side— there were seven, only one of them a boy. So I was looking forward to my first encounter with my lone paternal first cousin, a boy with a then-exotic-sounding name of Jean-Luc, who lived in far-off Paris.

That promise of a brief overseas trip turned out to be the first in a pattern of falsehoods my father told me regarding our emigration.

The significance of this subterfuge did not really dawn on me until decades later, when I reflected on his life after he died on August 25, 2010. In retrospect, I surmised that leaving Israel, the land of my birth and the place where my parents first met, turned out to be the first step in a long-term strategic plan to eventually reclaim what my father had lost during the Holocaust. As he stood beside me aboard the departing ship in Haifa, he could not have imagined that his grandiose plan would not be realized for another 35 years.

By 1957, my father had received confirmation from the International Red Cross that his parents had been murdered during the Nazi years. I did not know this at the time, but his quixotic quest for justice was centered on recouping the material losses the family had sustained during the war and, moreover, on restoring the reputation of the once prominent Gronner family name in his native Ilmenau, a German city nestled in a valley surrounded by the wooded hills of Thuringia.

Cruising toward Marseilles, I was unaware that my parents' intention was not merely a visit with my father's older brother, whom he had last seen before the outbreak of war in 1939. As it turned out, rather than return to Israel, my father, then thirty seven, hatched a plot to move the family to post-war Germany in order to reclaim German citizenship—one of the first benefits the guilt-ridden West German government extended to any Jewish citizen who had survived the atrocities in the death camps or successfully fled.

Since we never talked about it, I never found out why he thought it would be advantageous to reclaim German citizenship in 1957 at the height of the Cold War, when Ilmenau was still deep inside the Soviet-dominated part of Germany behind the Iron Curtain.

Unlike West Germany, the East at the time accepted no sense of official responsibility for Nazi war crimes, blaming them exclusively on the former "Fascist" regime in the part of Germany dominated by the victorious Western allies. In fact, the post-war Soviet-controlled German Democratic Republic saw itself as a victim of the fiercely anti-Communist pre-war Hitler government. Officially, state propaganda swept aside any responsibility for the acts of Nazi officials of my father's hometown; in fact, it was they who had incited the boycott and pogroms that preceded the so-called "Aryanization" of my grandparents' property; they were the ones to implement the order of my grandparents' deportation to certain death.

Whatever possessed my parents to settle in Frankfurt, it became clear to me that my mother's family members, and close friends of my parents, had made up their minds to leave Israel and seek opportunities in America. So, in the fall of 1959, just as I turned twelve, our family joined the Jecke exodus from Israel and headed to New York. My father had taken us out of the land of milk and honey and was leading us to one where the streets were paved with gold.

After my father died, I set out to research and recount his life story. The project is highly personal, though far from unique. Literally six million stories emanated from the smoke that rose from the crematoria and the killing fields that dotted the European countryside from 1939 to 1945. And though undisputed historical facts run through most accounts of the Holocaust, my intent here is not to bear witness. After all, I wasn't born until 1947. This is merely the story of a stubborn man whose dogged pursuit to correct the injustice visited upon him by anti-Semitism has indelibly shaped my own perspective. Having been spared the camps, he never referred to himself as a "survivor"; yet like the millions directly or indirectly affected by the terrible deeds of the Nazi regime, there is no denying the obvious.

It was inevitable that my father's first hand experience and outlook on family, fate, religion, politics, and the human condition would come to define me as well. With that realization, I reluctantly accepted my identity as a member of the "second generation," along with the concomitant duty of remembrance.

I am hardly alone in sharing this obligation. With the passing of that generation of survivors and first-hand eyewitnesses, the duty has passed to us post-war Baby Boomers. We, their children, cannot credibly testify to what happened in those dark years; yet we have seen the impact of the Holocaust on our survivor parents, despite their reluctance to openly address their inner regrets, pain, anger, and deep sense of loss. As I learned upon embarking on this task, it quickly became clear that few of my generation had truly explored the impact of the social convulsions visited upon their parents in their youth: dislocation, educational pursuit disrupted by war, and the loss of parents to guide their lives.

My objective here is to fill this void through the prism of my personal experience. I owe it to my American-born children and grandchildren to shed light on their heritage, and on my father's lifelong pursuit to reclaim a stolen past.

CHAPTER 1

Fleeting Frontiers

S EVERAL YEARS AGO, ANIMATED DIGITAL MAPS made the rounds on social media, condensing a thousand years of shifting European political borders into a matter of minutes. A virtual kaleidoscope of colors on the computer screen demonstrated the ephemeral nature of imaginary boundaries drawn by humans to reflect momentary victories, whether by war, subjugation or manifest destiny; possibly, these could have even have resulted from voluntary agreements to geographically divide populations by particular affinities—along tribal, familial, ethnic, religious, racial, linguistic, or political distinctions.

As proven through millennia, however, culture and heritage cannot be confined to lines on a map; inevitably the political wisdom or military might driving such decisions spawns simmering resentment, if not open conflict, among neighbors.

Live long enough, and you are likely to witness many changing frontiers over a lifetime. In the decades since my 1947 birth in Tel Aviv, I have lived through the emergence of a Jewish nation-state carved out of British Mandate Palestine, itself under English control as the spoils of the First World War against the Ottoman Turks.

In my lifetime, the disintegration of the Soviet Empire shattered the illusory "union" of the socialist "republics" that were held captive by the Moscow regime.

As noted by German novelist Peter Schneider, observing the events of 1989, "the virus of nationalism rages most fiercely in the Soviet republics, whose citizens, even women, children and the aged, are being killed simply because they belong to a different ethnic group. What does it all mean? Have we gone back to the 19th century? Have people freed themselves of Communism only to bend to the older yoke of national frenzy and race war? Or does this herald—at least in Europe—a new multicultural beginning, an 'internationalism" from below."[1]

Yet a mere twenty five years later, Vladimir Putin's Russia had again redrawn the Eastern European map with its seizure of Crimea from Ukraine, to the consternation of the Kiev government that had ousted its corrupt pro-Russian strongman, Viktor Yanukovych.

Yugoslavia, a polyglot nation that literally defined the term "balkanization", was ripped apart into its component parts immediately after the demise of the Tito dictatorship. Irrespective of his near three decades of ironclad control over the country, the long-suppressed ethnic, religious and linguistic rivalries, unfettered at the moment of his death in 1980, even precipitating documented genocide.

The Balkans of the 1990s were proof that the aggrieved losers never forget their perceived injustices, no matter how long their passions are smothered.

I was a mere eight months old when Israel declared its independence on May 15, 1948, triggering a coordinated military attack by the surrounding Arab armies committed to its destruction. The war (the Arabs refer to it as *Nakba*—the disaster) culminated in a United Nations-negotiated armistice. It established a temporary demarcation line for our national borders, placing the West Bank under Jordanian administration, and designating the twenty five-mile long Gaza Strip under Egyptian control.

By the time I reached school age, I understood that Israel was the homeland of the Jewish people. Everyone I knew was Jewish, my father recited Kiddush each Friday, and we celebrated all types of Jewish holidays, even though we never attended religious services in a synagogue. "Jewish" was seared into my essence and self-identification; as a kid, "Israeli" was an identity I was too young to understand.

When I was old enough to grasp the significance of frontiers between "the Arabs" and "us," the distinction became palpable during a visit to relatives in Jerusalem as I peered across a barbed wire fence into the no-man's land that divided the city's western and eastern halves. Even though I had learned about ancient Israel, I could not intellectually understand that the Jewish holy sites in the Old City were inaccessible to Israelis. To my eight-year-old mind, the other side of the barbed wire was merely another country, different from my own. Moreover, no Jews lived there.

After the Six Day War, which broke out a decade after my family emigrated from Israel, the victorious Israelis reunited the city of Jerusalem as the nation's capital and redrew the post-1948 armistice boundaries to enhance its defensive position. The so-called "Green Line" more or less delineates the frontier under a future peace pact with an envisioned Arab Palestinian nation. As of this writing, the "Final Status" of Jerusalem, now united (or arguably "occupied" in the eyes of Palestinians and their supporters), is still subject to debate as part of an envisioned "two-state" solution.

The stalemate to achieve lasting peace by two intractable visions held by people claiming their right to the same sliver of land remains unresolved. One side's self-determination continues to be cast as occupation by the other, and the chasm between them remains insurmountable.

In 1992, I joined my parents on a trip to Germany, where I again witnessed the impact of another man-made frontier separating people within their own land. By that time the physical separation that had locked residents of East Germany behind the so-called "Iron Curtain" had already been removed. But its vestiges were plainly evident as my father drove a rented car from Frankfurt to what had been the Communist side.

I had joined my parents at a favored resort hotel in the Taunus range of hills just north of Frankfurt. My father, an avid hiker in his youth, still enjoyed leisurely promenades once he reached his seventies, and I tagged along. The resort also had tennis courts, and I helped him practice for a tournament organized by the resort's activities director.

With my father driving a rented car, we headed east on the miracle of post-war Germany—the vaunted Autobahn—where no speed limits were posted at the time. I sat in the front passenger seat. My mother—all four foot ten of her—dozed in the back seat, barely reaching the bottom of the window to look out at the countryside flashing by.

The paved roadway abruptly ended at a point close to the one-time frontier, where we were diverted to local rural routes. The car slowed to a crawl as my father negotiated the vehicle around cobblestone streets where numerous potholes gave the appearance of a moonscape dotted with craters left by a thousand miniature asteroids. In contrast to the contemporary, red-roofed buildings I had seen whizzing by from the passenger side window on the Autobahn, I now saw whole villages of gray, decrepit structures that had not been tended to in decades.

"Look at that," I pointed out at one moment, seeing a small group of women lethargically wave their straw brooms over the cobblestones. Not a bit of litter was in sight, but there they were, kerchiefs covering their hair, sliding the bristles in robot-like fashion as if to demonstrate (to whom? I asked myself) that they were assiduously performing their assigned task for the State. Except the State no longer existed. Their status as street sweepers was still in limbo, the two governments still not having completed the onerous task of unifying their bureaucracies.

MY PERSONAL EXPERIENCE WITH TECTONIC SHIFTS in political boundaries was only the most recent in a series that my family faced, dating back to my grandfather's birth on January 12, 1885. Samuel Gronner, for whom I was named, was born in a Central European region called Silesia, at the time ruled as a dynastic duchy of the Austro-Hungarian Empire.

Silesia was situated along the major trading routes between Asia and Western Europe dating back millennia. Consequently, the region had historically been a pawn in the geopolitical chess match among feudal families and their successor empires. German-speaking Prussia and Austria, the dominant powers to the West and South, and Russia to the East, had ruled the area since the defeat of an independent Polish nation a century earlier.

Although Slavs constituted the majority of Austrian Silesia, ethnic Germans held the political and economic power in the urban area known as Teschen. By the end of the nineteenth century, Teschen Silesia was the most economically developed region in the Austro-Hungarian

Empire, becoming a center for textiles, in addition to wood furniture and publishing. Assimilated German-speaking Jews chose to align with the power center, which drew many Jews transplanted from neighboring Galicia, nearly doubling the Jewish population in the three decades prior to 1890.[2]

Jewish inhabitants in Teschen had enjoyed relative economic and religious security in comparison to those in neighboring Galicia and the Czarist-controlled eastern part of historic Poland at the time. The divergence in circumstances led to a concomitant perspective on Judaism itself, as I learned on a visit to Poland to research my grandfather's Silesian roots. In preparation for the visit, I had engaged the services of a local expert on Jewish genealogy, Jacek Proszyk, whose doctoral thesis drew an approximate line of demarcation that distinguished the beliefs and practices of Jews living east of the Biala River, and my grandfather's birthplace some twenty miles to the west.[3]

The Gronners were a product of the Jewish Enlightenment period known as the *Haskalah*, which was prevalent from the late 1700's to the nineteenth century. This strain of progressive Judaism, advocated by German philosopher and intellectual Moses Mendelssohn (1726-1789), echoed the general Enlightenment and Renaissance sweeping through Western Europe. Many Jews of German-speaking Austrian Silesia, including my forebears, adopted this assimilationist German-Jewish identity, which stressed the importance of a secular education and a liberal practice of Judaism, in contrast with the religion-centered yeshivas and Hasidic culture and Yiddish language that prevailed in neighboring Galicia and eastern Europe.

My grandfather was the second of ten children born to Hermann Gronner and his wife, the former Auguste Sonnenfeld. Samuel's birthplace was officially listed as Haslach, an agrarian village adjoining

Teschen—today called Cieszyn, Poland.

On my Cieszyn trip in 2014 to meet Jacek, the researcher, I took time to explore the old town. There was scant tourist information in English from the local tourist office on the main town square. But in walking around I learned that the original Teschen had extended across the River Olza, and that the victorious Allies in the First World War had split it in half, with the west bank of the river ceded to Czechoslovakia.

On that visit I also took a short drive to the Hazlaka, as Haslach is known today. During my drive, I found only a church and adjoining school and cemetery, but saw nothing to indicate any vestige of Jewish life. A chill enveloped me as daylight waned, so I climbed back into the car and ventured into a pub I spotted, set back from the road. There I encountered several men whose garb indicated they were local farmers. "Do you speak English?" I asked. Only the youngest among them responded in the affirmative.

"I am from America," I said. "My grandfather was born in Hazlaka in 1885, and I am trying to find out exactly where. Have you ever heard of the name Gronner?" The young man translated, but the name drew no familiarity from any of the men.

The bartender went to the back and emerged with a pamphlet. "Maybe this could help," the young man translated for him, clearly the eldest of the bunch. I could not read Polish, but the collection of photos indicated the pamphlet had been designed to commemorate the centennial of the founding of the local church.

"My family is Jewish," I pointed out. They all looked surprised, as if to say, "Jews? Here?" After a round of beers I thanked them for their hospitality and left. It led me to suspect that in 1885, when it was common practice, Auguste delivered Samuel with the help of a midwife who lived in Haslach.

I had made a date with Jacek Proszyk to meet at the Cieszyn office of the Polish National Archive. I was referred to him by the head archive office in Warsaw due to his reputation as a researcher of the former Jewish community in Bielsko-Biala. He has compiled a massive database of surnames of former Jewish residents from surviving Jewish cemeteries, as well as official records that escaped destruction during the Nazi occupation of Poland.

Among the records he showed me was a reproduction of a notebook cover with vertical stripes, which turned out to be the main register for the "Volksschule" (public school) in the city of Skotschau from 1894 to 1916. The listing included Samuel Gronner and his brother Immanuel, two years his junior, as registered students.

In light of what I had learned about *Haskalah*, it made perfect sense that Hermann and Auguste would want their children to attend the public school. For that purpose, they had settled in the town of Baumgarten, much closer to the city of Skotschau, which had a growing Jewish community that would reach three hundred by 1900.

The Skotschau school register that Jacek had unearthed disclosed that the then-nine-year-old Samuel and seven-year-old Immanuel previously had been attending the public primary school in Baumgarten, now known as Dębowiec. Their father Hermann was alternatively listed as "businessman" and "Innkeeper" in Baumgarten, some four miles to the east of Skotschau, now called Skoczów.

"Sami," as he came to be known in the family, was for the most part an average student, with his weakest grades in religion, industriousness, mathematics and Polish language. He was ranked high in reading, writing, and science. His teacher was most impressed with his moral behavior, for which he consistently received his highest grades. Exposure to public education from a very young age set the seeds for Sami's future civic consciousness.

Austrian Silesian Jews benefited from the turn-of-century economic activity, with many becoming merchants and bankers, and profiting from the hospitality industry. Jews were elected to municipal government. The most successful sent their children for university study in Vienna, from there entering the legal and medical professions.

The Gronner household grew crowded as seven more children were born to Hermann and Auguste: Rosa (Rose), Wilhelm, David, Margit (Margarete/Grete), Salomon (Salo), Leopold (Poldi) and Siegfried.

By the time he reached twenty-two, Samuel Gronner left Silesia and headed west to seek his fortunes in Germany.

CHAPTER 2

Family Enterprise

I N LATE SUMMER 2014 I received a surprising proposal from my son. "Hey, Pops," Jesse said on the call from Portland, Oregon. "I need to be in Spain for meetings. What if we hooked up in Germany afterward and took a trip down memory lane in Opa's home town?"

"Are you serious?" I asked incredulously.

"Absolutely. He spoke so much about Ilmenau. I'm sorry I didn't get a chance to go there with him, but now that he's gone, I'd like to see it with you and experience it for myself."

The timing was fortuitous. For at least five years, I had been mulling what to do with the contents of a dust-collecting carton on the closet floor in our guest bedroom that doubles as my office.

On an earlier visit to my parents' home in Florida, Aba had been re-luctantly consolidating the household effects that he would be unable to take to their next destination—an assisted living facility.

With a forlorn gaze, he had pointed to a foot-high stack of folders. "I no longer have use for this," he had told me. "It's now your legacy."

Family Enterprise

In the intervening years, I had occasionally flipped through some of the contents in the carton—photocopies of legal documents, letters (some tattered), hand drawn family trees, photos, and assorted memorabilia from my parents' travels to Germany. To the chagrin of my wife (who regularly hangs her freshly laundered clothes to dry in the closet) the unattended carton on the floor became a point of contention between us.

"What are you doing with this stuff? If you're not using it, let's just put it in our storage bin," she complained. Evidently, she had failed to hear the plaintive calls emanating from the box, beckoning me to do something with it.

Jesse's proposal was the catalyst to embark on the project of chronicling my father's story, beginning with the town that loomed so large in his life.

The plan was soon set. My son and I would meet in Frankfurt on Friday night, November 7 and he would return to his family in Portland, Oregon the following Wednesday. Though brief, our visit to Ilmenau would encompass the November 9 commemoration of Kristallnacht, marking the 1938 pogrom against Germany's Jewish population.

"Since we'll be back in Frankfurt I'm going to extend my European stay," I told him, explaining that I resolved to take a later flight that day to Krakow and drive to Cieszyn to see what I could find out about my grandfather's Silesian roots. From there, I told him, I will head for the Jewish Museum in Berlin.

"Four days is a very short visit," I cautioned my son when I outlined our itinerary. "But one person we absolutely must visit is Opa and Oma's friend Juliane."

Dr. Juliane Rauprich was the municipal historian my parents had gotten to know during their occasional visits to Ilmenau after German reunification.

My father described her as an extremely warm and friendly individual who openly shared information she had uncovered about Ilmenau's former Jewish community in the Gestapo files that had been preserved in East Germany after the war. Her original research, supplemented by interviews with survivors, had been published in 1999 in a German academic journal under the title, *Remembrances of the Jews from the City of Ilmenau.*[4]

My father corresponded with her regularly and always brought back photos from their get-togethers when he and my mother visited. She was among the first people I had corresponded with following my father's death, and I'd been in touch with her from time to time. So when I emailed her that I would be traveling to Germany with Jesse, she enthusiastically agreed to see us.

My mother was known to boast about her children and grandchildren, so when her son and grandson showed up at the modest home in Pösneck, a thirty-minute drive from Ilmenau, Juliane and her husband Wolfgang greeted us warmly, as if we had come for a family reunion.

"Why, they never told me you are as petite as my mother," I exclaimed. "No wonder you got along so well!" Such was our immediate rapport that I felt comfortable expressing what a stranger might easily misinterpret as an insult.

Our hosts could not have been more gracious as the four of us gathered around a large table in an airy salon, illuminated by the daylight that soaked the room from the surrounding windows. As the pleasantries and her ebullient reminiscences of my parents appeared endless, I became conscious of the passage of time before a planned lunch at the historic rathskeller (a typical regional gut-filling sauerbraten, potato and red cabbage). But before departing, I asked Juliane to show me some of her files related to the Jewish community.

This is how I discovered an important piece of the puzzle of how Samuel Gronner would eventually become a prominent member of Ilmenau's business, civic and Jewish communities.

MY FATHER AND I NEVER DISCUSSED how his father came to leave his native Silesia. Only after his passing did I find among my father's papers a photocopy of a document he had submitted, in the early nineteen sixties, to the East German authorities. Filling more than two single-spaced pages, it recounted in granular detail the milestones and financial circumstances to support his claim for restitution of property seized from the family during the Nazi era.

While comprehensive in making the case for financial compensation, the document shed little light on what had motivated a twenty-two-year-old to leave his birthplace and his family. I can only surmise that in leaving Austria for the German Reich, the young man had seen the potential for upward economic and social mobility, a foreshadowing of my own father's motivations exactly fifty years later in uprooting his wife and children for a new life abroad.

Like many Silesian Jews engaged in one of the region's major industries, Samuel's vocational focus was on textiles. According to the same document, in 1907 he landed a sales job in Ölsnitz, a Saxonian town where the drapery industry is vibrant until this day.

Most striking to me in the dry recitation of facts in the document was a matter-of-fact notation of an event that would seal the fate of the Gronner family for generations: that in 1910 Samuel landed a sales job at the Leschziner clothing shop in Ilmenau, nestled in a picturesque valley cut through the Thuringian Forest by the River Ilm.

The man who hired Samuel was also a Jewish migrant from the east.

Wilhelm Sandler, nine years Samuel's senior, hailed from Hohensalza, located in Posen, Prussia (now Poznan, Poland).

In relating the Sandler family history, I am relying heavily on the work of a pair of third-generation descendants of Wilhelm: his grandson, Peter Weil of Chicago, the author of a family memoir[5], and Yoram Grinspan, Wilhelm's grandnephew.

With the help of professional genealogists and personal visits, Yoram had uncovered material from the Polish National Archives tracing the family presence in Hohensalza to Wilhelm's grandfather Abraham, a cobbler, whose profession (Sandler, in Yiddish) came to be assigned to the family surname.

Born in 1808, Abraham had married Golde, six years his junior, a daughter of Louis and Ernestine Lewin. Abraham and Golde bore eight children, one of whom, Meyer, was born in 1832.

In 1857, Meyer Sandler married Chaye Schafransky and fathered five children: Ernestine, born in 1858; Louis, born in 1859; Samuel, born in 1861; Dora, born in 1863; and Neumann, born in 1865. Tragically, Chaye and the six-year-old Louis died after contracting cholera in 1866. The thirty-year-old Chaye left Meyer a widower at age thirty-four with four children aged eight and younger.

The Sandlers, as was typical of Jews in the eastern reaches of the German Empire, were more religiously observant than the Gronners, who, as I have explained, reflected the assimilationist tendencies prevalent in Austrian Silesia.

Like his father, Meyer was a cobbler professionally, but, being Orthodox, he also became a part-time teacher in the Beth Hamidrash, the local religious school.

I have seen a Sandler family heirloom—a photograph of the bearded Meyer, donning a Bucharian-style dark embroidered skullcap—that outwardly exhibits the stereotypical image of an Orthodox Jew. It always struck me as a stark contrast to Hermann Gronner, portrayed hatless and clean-shaven, except for a moustache, in the only available photo of my paternal great-grandfather.

Although traditional Jewish law requires a widower to marry an unmarried sister of his deceased wife, this does not appear to have occurred in the case of Meyer Sandler. Yoram's research did not disclose siblings other than Chaye's brother, Leyser Schafransky.

That may explain why on November 1, 1875, forty-three year-old Meyer Sandler married twenty-four year-old Rebeka (Rivka) Meyer, a young woman who had been preparing meals for his religious school students.

Having fathered four children with his first wife, Meyer started a new family with Rivka with the birth of Wilhelm in 1876. Over the years, Rivka bore ten additional Sandler children in Hohensalza, five of whom died at a very young age. The remainder of Wilhelm's siblings who survived to adulthood were Isidor, born in 1880; Paula, born in 1882; Helene, born in 1887, and Georg, born in 1892.

Wilhelm had come to the Bavarian city of Coburg in 1899 and was hired for a sales position in the headquarters of the regional Leschziner clothing store chain, located in the city's main business district at 21 Spitalgasse.

During the ensuing decade and a half, the shrewd and ambitious Wilhelm managed to acquire the Leschziner business, along with its tagline, *Das Fachgeschäft für gute Kleidung* (The specialty store for fine clothing). As orchestrated by Wilhelm by virtue of his ingenious formula for blending family fealty and skillful matchmaking, it was the beginning of a family enterprise with stores in multiple locations.

AMONG THE MANY FILES I PERUSED in Juliane Rauprich's home was a roster of Jewish financial backers of the local institution called the Beteraum, a prayer room that the local congregation regularly used for religious observances, even though the community lacked a full time rabbi.

While Samuel Gronner was included on the roster, another name stood out for me: Isidor Abraham. Yoram's research of the Sandler heritage had disclosed that Ernestine, a half-sister from Meyer Sandler's first marriage, had married a Simon Abraham and bore a son they had named Isidor.

How is it that Isidor from Prussia came to be living in Ilmenau? I wondered. It stood to reason that Willi had arranged for his nephew—the son of his half-sister, and eight years younger—to oversee the Leschziner branch he had acquired.

From what I had already known about my grandparents, seeing the name of Isidor Abraham among the *Beteraum* supporters filled in a missing piece in the puzzle of how the fates of Samuel Gronner and Wilhelm Sandler became entwined: Wilhelm had devised a business expansion strategy that relied on the people he trusted most—namely, members of his extended family. It is a formula that eventually led Samuel, the young man who came west in pursuit of his dream for success, to be absorbed into the Sandler clan.

To execute his scheme, Wilhelm, a bachelor, initially invited his teenaged sister Paula to join him in Coburg to be his homemaker.

Having someone reliable manage the home front, Willi turned his attention to his satellite stores. What if he could find an eligible partner for his sister to manage the Leschziner store in Sonneberg? Thus he turned matchmaker for Paula and one of his salesmen, Bernhard Grünspan. With Wilhelm's blessing, the couple married in 1903, upon Paula's reaching the age of twenty-one. Bernhard and Paula settled in Sonneberg and operated that branch he had acquired.

His success inspired Willi to repeat his formula, and he invited his other sister, Helene, to be his homemaker in Coburg. In the interim, Willi was drawn to a young woman, Selma Kaufmann, whom he would marry in 1908 after a protracted engagement. Selma assisted Willi in the store, keeping the books, managing inventory and helping with sales, while Helene minded the home front as housekeeper and cook.

After being hired in 1910, Samuel shared the apartment with Isidor Abraham across a courtyard behind the Wilhelm Sandler store on what was then called Poststrasse.

With no relatives nearby, Samuel no doubt accompanied Isidor, Wilhelm's nephew, to the Sandlers' family events in Coburg, or to Paula and Bernhard Grünspan's home in Sonneberg, providing an opportunity for Samuel to befriend Helene. It did not take long for the pair to develop a romantic relationship, prompting Wilhelm to make his next move. He asked Isidor to open another Wilhelm Sandler affiliate in Mühlhausen, some fifty miles to the north.

This set the stage for Samuel's promotion to branch manager in Ilmenau. Then, on May 16, 1911, Wilhelm oversaw the wedding of his sister Helene to Samuel Gronner. As the *de facto* patriarch of the family, the eldest brother's dowry most likely included transfer of ownership of the store to the newlyweds, but retained its brand name, Wilhelm Sandler.

With guidance from Willi, the young couple began to grow its customer base by focusing on mens' and boys' clothing, specializing in quotidian urban garb and merchandise suited for the many tradespeople in town and its outskirts. In the document recounting the origins of his claim for compensation, my father reported that the business grew to such an extent that his parents rented an adjoining storefront on Posstrasse within three years.

But this was a time of simmering international intrigue. Italy had invaded and seized Libya as a North African defensive post across the Mediterranean, and the Balkans erupted into war in an attempt by nationalist factions to shed the yoke of the Ottoman Turks. Yet in Ilmenau, business boomed for the handful of Jewish businesses owned by my family, along with those of the Eichenbronners and Gabbes.

It did not take long for Sami and his wife Lenchen (her name within the family) to relocate to larger and modernized quarters at No. 8 Poststrasse, with a refurbished residence above the shop. The expanded business prospered, and the family grew with the arrival of a son, named Rudolf, on February 12, 1912.

In the summer of 1914 Germany was part of the Central Powers Alliance waging the First World War against the Allied Powers consisting of Great Britain, France, Russia, Italy, Romania, Japan and the United States. With her husband conscripted into the army, Lenchen was burdened with caring for a two-year-old Rudy and managing the family business. Selma, her sister-in-law, took charge of the Coburg store while Willi was on active duty.

Despite these challenges, in 1916 Helene obtained documentation that allowed her and Rudy to pass through the Austrian frontier. Her purpose is unclear in my mind. The caption of a photo accompanying Juliane Rauprich's obituary of my father stated that Helene intended to visit her husband at the front. This seemed implausible to me. My theory is that she was bound for Vienna, the Austrian capital where her husband's kin had resettled.

During my 2014 visit with Jesse, we were treated to a VIP tour of the offices of Ilmenau's municipal archives. Martina Arnold, the friendly and accommodating director, had printed out a summary report of family-related records in her files that she had meticulously bound with string. She then escorted us to a table where she had proudly displayed the pièce de résistance: the original travel document featuring a striking photo of Helene, sporting a high-collared light colored blouse, with the young Rudy leaning on her shoulder. What amazed me is that the document, still pristine, had miraculously survived two world wars, including the destructive Nazi years, and been further preserved by the secretive East German regime.

Upon returning from the front after the war in 1918, Samuel was awarded the Iron Cross for his military service—a symbol he would later invoke to no avail when Nazi sympathizers raised doubt about his patriotism because of his Jewish faith. (Many years later, when the grandfather in the 1978 Holocaust TV miniseries was portrayed wearing the Iron Cross, it reminded my father of his own dad, whose effort to exude pride in being German proved for naught.)

The First World War left Germany's economy in shambles, yet for shop owners, the resulting inflation meant higher valuation in net worth as calculated in the devalued Reichsmark. The emergence of the postwar Weimar Republic initially generated optimism that a democratic Germany would prosper in the long run. Berlin's "Roaring Twenties" lit afire, as a cultural revolution spread through the country with innovations in art, music and dance. Significantly, the revolutionary *Bauhaus* architectural style was spawned in nearby Weimar.

On May 7, 1920, Helene gave birth in the living quarters above the store on Poststrasse. The second son was named Joachim Heinz Gronner—my father.

CHAPTER 3

Inspiration to Action

AFTER A LONG DAY WITH JULIANE AND WOLFGANG, we spent Saturday night in a B&B I had found online. The Franzenshof was, as advertised, "a Franconian three-sided court built around 1740" that had "been lovingly restored bit by bit since the mid-1990s."

The description was apt if limited to the exterior wattle-and-daub finish reflecting its eighteenth century provenance, but it omitted a detail relevant to present-day overnight guests: the interior furnishing could only be described as "contemporary Ikea," wherein my hastily assembled bed collapsed on itself and the mattress landed flat on the "lovingly restored" floor—with me on it! It did not deter me from getting a good night's rest. My jet-lagged body needed sleep, so I just stayed on the mattress where it had landed.

On Sunday morning, after an unremarkable breakfast, we headed to our next destination. Aware that our itinerary would include spending November 9 in Germany, I had asked Juliane, even before departing for

Europe, "Do you know whether there are any events planned to mark Kristallnacht while we're in Ilmenau?"

"The Thüringen Jewish community will conduct a commemoration at the memorial to Holocaust victims in the Jewish cemetery in Erfurt," she told me. "And usually there is a vigil in Ilmenau in the evening."

Relying on my GPS-equipped mobile phone, Jesse helped with the navigation to the Jewish Cemetery, and we arrived with time to spare before the official ten o'clock start. People were filing in, in pairs and clusters, forming a semi-circle around the memorial unto which a fresh coat of gold paint had been applied to highlight the words etched in the stone, "In memory of our murdered brothers and sisters, 1933–1945."

Wreaths festooned in crimson tail flowers, yellow gerbera daisies, mums and carnations commingled in white and red had been placed on stands facing the assembled, an explosion of color contrasting with the charcoal-colored stone of the memorial to the rear.

The number of participants swelled to several dozens—perhaps eighty people—and I could clearly make out that the vast majority were chatting quietly in Russian. Such is the contemporary Jewish demography of Thuringia, I thought to myself.

A man with close-cropped snow-white hair, whose chiseled, pointed nose, full-moon face, and ice blue eyes telegraphed his VIP status by making the rounds greeting acquaintances. He then approached Jesse and me—a pair of unrecognizable faces in the otherwise familiar crowd. This was Professor Dr. Reinhard Schramm, the head of the Jewish Federation of Thuringia, in his finest politico mode.

"An honor to meet you, sir," I addressed him in German. "I am Sam Gronner from the United States and this is my son, Jesse. My grandparents lived in Ilmenau before they were deported. We came here today to memorialize them."

"Ah, Herr Gronner, so wonderful you could make it. Yes, I was advised we would have dignitaries from the United States with us today. Thank you for joining us," he said as he proceeded on his rounds of glad-handing.

Dignitaries? Jesse and I gave each other a baffled look.

Sure enough, moments later, after a benediction by Alexander Zakharenko, the bearded Russian-born cantor, Herr Dr. Schramm stepped up to the lectern which had been set up alongside the memorial, and proceeded to welcome the panoply of Thuringian officials standing beside him—among them the state's justice minister, the mayor of Erfurt, political party spokespeople—and yes, pointing in my direction, Herr Gronner from the United States.

As the speakers stepped to the mic for their remarks, I quietly whispered fragments of translations to Jesse so he might at least get an understanding of what was being said. The overarching message, in light of current events (still ongoing), was a call to reject bigotry and hateful persecution of Muslim refugees, applying the lesson that the Shoah happened because the majority of Germans failed, through apathy or fear, to challenge the early manifestation of hate with the pogrom of the night of November 9, 1938.

JEWS WHO HAD FLED NAZI GERMANY for the most part continued to speak their native language upon arrival in Palestine, except for those who, because of their experience, vowed never to utter a German word again, along with a pledge never to buy another German product—most notably cars.

When I am asked what languages I speak, I always make the point that, even though I grew up in Hebrew-speaking Israel, German was my first language. That was the language in which I conversed with my mother, beginning when I was a toddler, right up to the last day I saw her alive in her wheelchair, a blank look on her face as she struggled to find a word after the stroke she had suffered at age ninety-two.

I never really progressed much beyond the conversational German I was exposed to in my family of *Jeckes*. The moniker has a dubious etymology in stereotypical portrayals of German-speaking immigrants who donned a formal jacket (*Jacke*) for virtually any type of social event, as though they were still living in Berlin or Vienna instead of the sweltering Middle East. The image of the well-dressed ladies having their *Kaffeklatsch* in the outdoor cafés of Hayarkon Street and Dizengoff Circle in Tel Aviv is seared in my memory.

My ability to converse in German—and comprehend some complex legal terminology with the help of Google Translate—has been an immense help in poring over the pile of documents I fondly refer to as "the museum" I inherited from my father. (It was certainly sufficient for my understanding of the speeches we had witnessed in Erfurt.)

German has been described as a language of words coupled like rail cars to form a train. A striking example is the name of the postwar department that the East German government established to hold in escrow private property and other assets that Jews had been forced to transfer to non-Jews under the Nuremberg Law. The term *Amt für Vermögungsfragen* literally translates to "Department for Questions Related to Assets." Employing the artifice of the German language, bureaucrats had created the functional term by coupling the word *Vermögen* (asset) with *Fragen* (questions).

In the colloquial German that I spoke at home, I had no reason to ever use the patois of bureaucratic and legal terminology that I encountered in my research. Moreover, the cursive handwriting of the period had exhibited highly individualized and regional characteristics, with decorative embellishments and curlicues that I failed to decipher. Even the periodicals and books of the time used in my research proved a challenge because they employed elaborate German Gothic typefaces.

To my relief, Yoram Grinspan and Peter Weil had already completed much of the spadework to chronicle the Sandler saga. But I would have gotten nowhere with the Gronner family history in Ilmenau had Jesse and I not made a new acquaintance that November day of consequence, which for all Germans marked not only the events of November 9, 1938 but also the exact date when East and West Germans breached the Berlin Wall in 1989.

The Erfurt memorial service concluded with Cantor Zakharenko's rendition of *El Maleh Rachamim*, the traditional Jewish prayer for the dead. Having time to spare before heading to Ilmenau, Jesse and I ventured to the well-preserved medieval part of the Erfurt. The narrow roadways limit access to residents and commercial vehicles only, so we found a parking spot outside the walled enclave and strolled in, guided by the Google Maps app on my phone. We soon found a bar that was just opening for the day.

A short respite over beer drawn from the tap sufficed to refresh us before a walk to the ancient synagogue, no longer a house of worship but a museum for local artifacts and a collection of rare coins unearthed during the excavations that had revealed its historic architecture. I was struck by the evidence of a Jewish presence in Germany dating back to the middle ages, exposing the falsehood spread during the Nazi era that German Jews were alien interlopers.

Later that afternoon we drove to Ilmenau, where I had booked a room in the Lindenhof Hotel. There, a rail-thin man in his fifties, soft spoken and formal, had come to visit us, introducing himself as Rainer

Borsdorf. Speaking virtually flawless English for Jesse's benefit, he informed us that he was representing the team of volunteers who had undertaken that year's annual commemoration of what Germans refer to as *Reichspogromnacht*. The name Kristallnacht, as commonly used in America, had fallen into disfavor in Germany because it glossed over the horrific terror campaign against Germany's Jewish population on the night of November 9, 1938.

Unbeknownst to me until then, he had been alerted to our arrival by Juliane Rauprich. Her information had set him in motion to orchestrate a set of experiences for my son and me to rival an itinerary for a state visit by foreign dignitaries—to wit the special attention we were given in the cemetery earlier in the day.

Although he held no formal title in the city, I learned that he had become Juliane's *de facto* successor, ensuring that the story of Ilmenau's former Jewish neighbors not be forgotten.

As arranged, we met Rainer and his team for a walking candlelight tour that passed several locations relevant to the history of the former Jewish community.

The chilly November evening, accompanied by a steady breeze, caused me to bundle up in an insulated ski parka and to warm my ears by pulling down the woolen ski cap I had packed. Still, I was impressed that about two dozen Christian participants had given up their Sunday evening to memorialize former Jewish neighbors who had died long before they were born.

In most cases, the procession led to a spot in front of a building where inscribed brass plates bearing the names of the murder victims, all former Jewish residents, were inlaid in the surrounding cobblestones on the sidewalk.

These four-inch square *Stolpersteine* are the creation of Gunter Demnig, an artist who conceived the project in 2000 to place "tripping stones" so that anyone passing the former home or business of a Holocaust victim would be forced to read the inscribed name, consistent with the Talmudic teaching that "a person is only forgotten when his or her name is forgotten."

At each stop along the walk, different students from the local high school read a brief biography of the former occupants that he or she had prepared based on personal research. Save for the light breeze, no other sound was detectable in the deserted street to distract attention from the solemn moment. The words of remembrance from the students' mouths became eerily enveloped in their vaporized breath, visibly emanating into the chilly air and dissipating like a cloud.

It was as if the students' utterances at each location had risen above the streets of my father's hometown, collecting like a layer of dew atop rooftops, a residue of the souls that had been snuffed out by the inhumanity perpetrated by neighbor against neighbor.

As people took turns laying flowers and lighting a memorial candle at each of the *Stolpersteine* on our route, I resolved to complete the mission begun by my father.

I would tell his story so that the other young people in Ilmenau and beyond would come to know the name of a family that the Nazi regime tried to obliterate. Moreover, I would find ways to use the story to inspire them to immediately recognize and counteract verbal expressions of bias, stereotyping, bullying and violence directed at people who are different from themselves.

As it turned out, Rainer Borsdorf would become my comrade in arms in completing my father's mission.

CHAPTER 4

Sunshine Ahead,
With Gathering Clouds

MONG THE MANY IMAGES DISCOVERED in my research is a vintage black and white photograph that captures the economic comfort the Sandler-Gronner-Grünspan clan had achieved by the mid-1920s. It is a moment of carefree relaxation, a family get-together, as the various aunts and uncles and their children reunite for their annual respite.

The whole lot, all clad in swimwear, are arrayed on the Baltic seashore, a patch of sand that Peter Weil had identified in his memoir as a favored Jewish resort of the extended Sandler clan—including Willi, his wife Selma and their daughter Ruth. This was also a place frequented by the family of Fritz Weil, his father and Ruth's husband.

Right there in the front row are the Gronner foursome: Sami, sheen sunlight reflecting off his hairless crown, his right arm lovingly wrapped around Helene's shoulder; next to them Jochen, as their younger son was called within the family, a mop of curls dangling over his ears; and the pre-teen Rudy, photo-model handsome, sitting back to back against his rotund uncle Willi, whose arms interlock with his daughter Ruth, seemingly engaged in a mutual staring contest.

Among the other cast of characters is Willi's other sister Paula and her husband Bernhard, owners of the family-affiliated store in Sonneberg, with two of their children, Rachel (whom everyone called Recha) and Heinz; their missing son Siegfried is presumably the photographer. Also in the photo is Willi's brother, the attorney Georg Sandler, on vacation with his family from Königsberg in East Prussia.

The photo literally captures a snapshot in time of a free-wheeling and democratic Germany, the period referred to as the Weimar Republic, governed by a civilian administration founded by a coalition of liberal political parties in 1918. It was one day after the abdication of the monarch, Kaiser Wilhelm, whom both Sami and Willi served in uniform, and for whom Willi's brother Isidor Sandler had given his life.

The newfound freedom after Germany's defeat in the First World War launched a virtual explosion of innovations in cultural expression, with a vibrant night life in Berlin's cabarets, a breakthrough contrarian art movement away from impressionism to a "New Objectivity," and a revolutionary architectural and design *Bauhaus* style that emerged from the city of Weimar, less than forty miles from Ilmenau.

But lurking on the horizon, invisible in this photo, a dark cloud is approaching. Much has been written about the failed experiment in civilian rule and political instability that characterized Weimar Germany. Burdened by the onerous reparation payments imposed by the victorious allies, the fledgling republic faced an enormous financial crisis from the outset.

The new government's shortsighted decision to stimulate economic activity by printing more money initially had a positive effect on small businesses like the Wilhelm Sandler enterprise. Cheaper money encouraged business investment. But with Germany's inability to quickly revive its major industries and generate the necessary revenues, hyperinflation set in. People eventually resorted to using the worthless Reichsmark notes as wallpaper.

To save the government from imminent collapse, the United States, represented by its budget director, Charles Dawes, devised a plan in 1923 to reform the national bank, issue new bank notes, and extend the repayment terms on the international debt.

Through this period the political climate remained unsettled, with the humiliated military class and ultranationalists vying to defeat the social democrats in charge.

Germany's well-assimilated Jewish population—my family among them—was squeezed between supporting the monarchists and militarists on one side, and, on the other, by Communist partisans inspired by the revolutionaries who had created a worker-dominated Soviet utopia by overthrowing the Romanoff Empire.

Given his upbringing and world view, there was no doubt that Samuel's only choice in confronting the conundrum facing German Jews was to do his part to bolster the forces of democracy, having concluded that any extremist position—whether on the left or right—would not be in the best interests of his family and the Jewish community.

It took the insight and initiative of my new comrade-in-arms Rainer Borsdorf to provide the proof to my hypothesis. In the process I discovered how similar Rainer's and Samuel's life experiences shaped identically reached conclusions about the power of democracy in securing individual human rights.

As I have already reported, Sami's primary school teacher had found him to possess a strong moral compass even at age nine. What's more, his parents' decision to enroll him in public school rather than giving him a sectarian yeshiva upbringing inculcated a robust sense of civic consciousness in him.

As I began collaborating with Rainer, he struck me as someone who was made of the same moral fiber and possessed the same sense of civic duty as Samuel Gronner had. In Rainer's case, these qualities are rooted in his authentic Christian values. I came upon that immediate impression when he presented me with an autographed copy of his newly published pamphlet, *Light and Shadow*, an unvarnished examination of Nazi ideology that had been tolerated—even openly supported—by Germany's Protestant churches, including the clergy and congregation of historic St. Jacobus Church in Ilmenau.

The introductory text, written by Angelika Greim-Harland, superintendent of the Arnstadt-Ilmenau district of the Evangelical Church, spoke volumes in summarizing Rainer's perspective of the German church dating back to the Reformation:

> The Jewish rabbi and mystic Ben Eliezer said, "Forgetting leads to exile; the mystery of salvation is remembrance. . . ."
> It pains me that the clergy of our church were also susceptible to Nazi ideology. I wish for a future church that can mourn the sacrifices of violence, consistent with the biblical message of forgiveness and the spirit of the times, courageously bringing the image of God's new world into view, in which all men are equal before God and have the dignity that no one can take from them.[6]

Over the course of the day following the solemn vigil to mark *Reichspogromnacht*, Rainer's formal earnestness with his foreign visitors rapidly evolved into camaraderie. He and his team had organized an agenda filled with activities—among them the visit to the municipal archives where the original travel document bearing the photo of my grand-mother and Rudy was put on display for our benefit. (I had noticed that he had included a copy in the newly printed pamphlet he had given me.) We were treated to a pleasant lunch hosted by the mayor, Oberbürger-meister Seeber, followed by an invigorating afternoon hike up to the *Bob-hütte*, a hut atop Ilmenau's renowned bobsled run.

We cemented our friendship the evening before our departure when I invited Rainer back to our room. Impressed by his assiduousness and genuine desire to bond with his American Jewish visitors, I deemed it appropriate to pop the inevitable question: "I have been thinking for a long time of a way to tell the story of my family. Would you be able to help me?"

A published author and historian, he looked at me quizzically. "What do you have in mind?"

"I'm not quite sure. Like you, I am a writer, and I have journalism experience. So perhaps I could write a book. But we live in the digital age," I noted, "and I think I need to think more broadly, perhaps using digital media that young people today tend to favor. Something inter-active that includes text and graphics—even audio."

Rainer's face lit up. "This is exactly what I had in mind," he ex-claimed. "Young people need to remember the former Jewish neighbors and learn how they were driven out of Ilmenau so that this crime is not repeated. But today, it's best to tell the story in an engaging, interactive way that appeals to young people."

We pledged to stay in touch and follow through on the idea once I was back home.

As I got to know Rainer over the years, I came to understand why and how he had veered in his career toward activism, writing, organizing events, and challenging anti-democratic ideology.

It stands to reason, given his life experience. Born in Dresden, Rainer spent his youth under the stifling environment of the East German Democratic Republic (GDR), where freedom of speech and thought were firmly controlled by the Socialist Party and enforced by agents of the Ministry of State Security—the despised Stasi—many of whom included neighbors.

At age nineteen, he graduated as a toolmaker from a vocational training program at a state owned electrical engineering enterprise in Dresden, and beginning in 1987 attended a specialized school to become certified in information research and documentation.

Two years into his studies, at age twenty-two, Rainer lived through the fall of communism and the obliteration of the fortifications that had kept East Germans locked inside their own country for fear of being executed while attempting to escape, as more than one thousand had tried to and failed.[7]

By sheer coincidence, upon reaching the age of twenty-two, Rainer Borsdorf and Samuel Gronner had breached similar symbolic frontiers, in each case marking the start of a new phase in their respective lives.

Germany's reunification blew a breath of fresh air into the oxygen-deprived prison of the former GDR, freeing Rainer to pursue his passions for intellectual inquiry into history and religion. This led him to the Friedrich Schiller University in Jena, which awarded him a master's degree in contemporary and medieval history and art in 2004.

Since then, he has pursued a career in freelance writing and research, primarily for church-affiliated organizations, but also editing monographs. He has worked for publishing houses and historical institutions like Buchenwald and Topf & Söhne, formerly the Erfurt-based producer of the specialized high-capacity ovens for Hitler's death camps. Additionally, under a pseudonym, he wrote a book on the development of the right-wing extremism that took root in the former East Germany.

Why the interest in such a niche specialty? I asked him. He confided that he'd become incensed upon discovering that his grandfather had been a Nazi party member. "This revelation has caused me to fight all forms of extremism, to promote democratic values, and to perpetuate the lessons of the Shoah. All this is required of me as a Christian whose faith teaches that all people have the same rights and whose lives are of equal worth."

Although I had known that Samuel Gronner had managed the finances of the congregation that conducted worship in Ilmenau's prayer room, it was Rainer who found proof that my grandfather had initiated an early grassroots effort in Ilmenau to strengthen the nascent Weimar democracy in order to guard against anti-Semitism.

In his online research, Rainer had come across an exchange of correspondence in the archives of the Central Union of German Citizens of the Jewish Faith, founded in Berlin in 1893 to protect the rights of Jews who saw their first allegiance to the German Reich. The so-called CV gained renewed relevance and impetus almost immediately upon the creation of the democratic Weimar Republic—my grandfather among those drawn to its mission. Tellingly, by 1927, CV membership had swelled to 70,000 and won the support of most assimilated German Jews.[8]

Rainer had discovered a memorandum dated April 3, 1923, noting that, in a conversation with a certain Herr Seefeld, described as an official of the organization, "Herr S. GRONNER in Ilmenau, Thür. seeks the establishment of a local group in Ilmenau, and further observes that after the launch, an additional fifteen paying participants would join."

Presciently, my grandfather had foreseen the Jewish federation's role as a protector of civil rights and a bulwark against bigotry spewed by an obscure fanatic named Adolf Hitler.

Within seven months after the memo, the Nazis used the fifth anniversary of Kaiser Wilhelm's abdication, November 8, 1923, to attempt an overthrow the Weimar Republic. The unsuccessful Putsch landed Hitler in jail, but in his eight months of incarceration, he managed to write *Mein Kampf*, a manifesto that led millions to follow his ideas.

CHAPTER 5

Leaving the Homeland

O N DECEMBER 18, 1996, my father sat down in my parents' bright living room in Coconut Creek, Florida, for an extensive video recorded discussion with Marvin Greenberg, a volunteer interviewer for Survivors of the Shoah Visual History Foundation, a project founded by the director Steven Spielberg.

The story he tells, preserved for posterity as Interview Number 24356, begins with his recollection of the rare occasions he had spent as a child in Ilmenau's prayer room behind the house at Number 4 Burgstrasse, owned by a Mrs. Zunge.

"The earliest memories I have from my childhood are the days— very few—spent in the prayer room. I saw my father wearing a white embroidered yarmulke, and my mother wearing her best clothes," he recalls. There was a lot of what he describes as "chitchat" among the grownups.

The congregation, which numbered 80 members by 1932, defined itself as a social community of like-minded Germans who practiced Jew-

ish rituals but who were outwardly like many of their non-Jewish neighbors. The members had formed their own bowling club, for example.

On the basis of her many interviews with witnesses like my father,
Juliane Rauprich had confirmed how Jews identified themselves in a
chapter in the sixth volume of a collection titled *Jews in South Thuringia:*

> *In all my conversations with children and grandchildren of that generation*
> *from the end of the nineteenth and beginning of the twentieth centuries, the*
> *founding principle of the local Jewish community clearly was that members re-*
> *garded themselves foremost as Germans, yet also as Germans of the Jewish faith.*
> *In the first third of our century, the families of Seligmann and Samuel Gronner*
> *were considered to be Jewish, albeit modestly. Although Shabbat was observed*
> *in almost every family, Rosh Hashanah and other High Holidays were cele-*
> *brated together, and most children were sent to Jewish religious education.[9]*

"I never went to kindergarten," my father notes in his video testimony, "but I did have a woman take care of me at five in the afternoon
because my mother helped my father in the department store."

When he entered first grade, my father, like virtually every German
child, participated in the national ritual of the *Zuckertüte*, where on the
first day of a child's schooling each brings a large cone filled with sugary
treats for a party. Despite the joyous atmosphere, when his mother
brought him to school, "I remember how frightened I was," he said in
describing his emotion and insecurity about how his life would change
from his sheltered experience at home.

"This was my first encounter with children who were not exactly
friendly." Recalling the curly tresses he sported in the family snapshot
on the Baltic beach, he reported his initial introduction to anti-Semitism
when his six-year-old classmates taunted him as a "Jew girl" for his

bobbed haircut.

Non-conformity was increasingly frowned upon in the prevalent nationalistic environment, and after more than a year of taunts, my grandparents relented and allowed their younger son to get a masculine haircut like the other boys.

I found it odd that in relating his childhood memories, my father does not mention the significant change in the family fortunes that led the family to relocate to larger quarters for their store and living quarters. I expected that his narrative would mention its impact on him. Yet in his video testimony he only makes a passing remark about the sixteen people his parents employed. Nonetheless, I know that the relocation would figure large in my father's later life.

The year 1930 would mark a confluence of events drawing the outlines of the fate that befell the Gronner family. For ten-year-old Jochen, it would mean moving on from the primary grades after passing a qualification for the *Goetheschule*, the picturesque school built next to a pond on a forested hill overlooking Ilmenau.

At about the same time, Thuringia held an election for the regional legislature—created as part the federation of semi-autonomous regions that the Weimar Republic had carved out of the pre-war royal entities of the German Reich.

As part of their election campaign, the Nazis organized demonstrations throughout Thuringia to underscore their "No Jews" platform and calling for a boycott Jewish businesses. The head of Ilmenau's chapter was Fritz Sauckel, a rabid anti-Semite who found himself in front of the Wilhelm Sandler store, where a confrontation ensued with my grandfather. The normally restrained Samuel Gronner lost his temper at the sight and sound of the roaring Sauckel in front of the shop and struck him in the face.[10] This act of defiance would make my grandfather a marked man for the rest of his life.

To the chagrin of my family, the Nazi Party took control of the legislature and named Sauckel as Germany's first anti-Semitic regional head of state. Wilhelm Frick, another well-known anti-Semite and Hitler ally, was named prime minister of Thuringia, and Willy Marschler, a sales clerk from Ilmenau, was appointed minister of education.

It was not long thereafter that my father recalled a particular Saturday, a school day, when all students were ordered into the school auditorium. There, the principal read a speech mandated by the new authorities, which included a recitation of a section of the Versailles Treaty. Article 231 states:

> *The Allied and Associated Governments affirm and Germany accepts the responsibility of Germany and her allies for causing all the loss and damage to which the Allied and Associated Governments and their nationals have been subjected as a consequence of the war imposed upon them by the aggression of Germany and her allies.*

The Nazis called this section a lie that had been imposed on the German Reich solely as an excuse for the onerous reparations. Hence, when Nazis took control of the regional government, they launched mandatory indoctrination in the schools. "If you recite this often enough," my father commented, "it sinks in, whether it's true or not, and you become convinced that Germany did not start the First World War. Rather it was the enemy."

It didn't take long for students to make anti-Semitic remarks to his face.

"My parents, like many Germans steeped in German culture, sought to sluff off these expressions as meaningless chatter. But to this day I do not see a distinction between idle speech and malevolent expression of anti-Semitism.

"Obviously, the generation before was far more tolerant in such matters," my father said of those days. "My parents really felt that this is nothing to be concerned about, as if it was just part of daily life, that I have to accept it as something normal. In hindsight, I feel that this was the route of evil."

When pressed by the interviewer for specific threats, my father demurred. Still, he cited "a pig of Jew" as a common epithet he heard, along with "blood-sucking Jew."

While the verbal taunts were evident during my father's grammar school days, he tended to dismiss the physical aggression and hazing as a typical dynamic among childish scamps, referred to in German as *Lausbuben*. But once he was at the *Goetheschule*, he felt the direct effects of the Nazi influence in the way anti-Semitism manifested itself in school.

Germany held national elections in November 1932, and the Nazi Party won 196 seats in the Reichstag. While this was short of a majority, President Paul von Hindenburg relied on Adolf Hitler to form a government by appointing him Chancellor on January 30, 1933. Less than a month later, the parliament building was set ablaze, and the Nazi Party and its allies convinced Hindenburg the state was under mortal threat, leading him to suspend all civil rights. The Nazi goal of turning Germany into a Fascist state was effectively completed.

THE EFFECT OF THIS NATIONAL UPHEAVAL on Jochen Gronner was almost immediate. School recess or lunch periods became a daily source of confrontation. "When I went to the schoolyard for recess, perhaps to eat a sandwich or talk to my schoolmates, there wasn't a day when I wasn't roughed up by compatriots," he recalled.

"Among 670 students enrolled, I was the only Jew. It started with being accosted, being called names, and culminated in a fistfight. I was never one to take an insult. So I fought back and quite often came home with a bloody shirt. My mother and father had both seen it."

Anti-Jewish state-sponsored propaganda took hold in the homes of many of my father's schoolmates and, with notable exceptions, also affected the faculty and administration.

One who did not toe the party line was the French teacher, Dr. Götze. "I knew him very well because he was a friend of my father. He was an active member of the German Democratic Party who served as an officer in the Prussian army during the war. I admired him as a man who was outstanding in any respect and as a true representative of humanism as expressed by Schiller and Goethe."

At war's end, Russian forces suspected that the French teacher was either a Nazi or someone who supported Nazism, and shipped him to Siberia. In his videotaped interview, my father states, "I was later approached by a friend of mine who survived the war, asking whether I would attest to Dr. Götze's anti-Nazi convictions at the time I was in school so he could be released from custody. I was glad to do it."

He added: "Strange, even during those Nazi times, there were dedicated teachers who could inspire, like Dr. Götze, from whom I learned French well."

My father described the chemistry teacher, Dr. Löhle, as an anti-Nazi who, to get around the requirement to give the Nazi greeting before class, waved his arm in a mock salute to the Führer. Another instructor, the math teacher Klee, was also a memorable character, proudly German but not a Nazi. A former Prussian officer and pro-monarchist, he had apparently suffered a sword injury to the mouth. "His scars extended from either end of his mouth, limiting his ability to open it completely, and anything he said sounded like a military command," my father said, mimicking the disability.

"I remember him well because he was a founding member of a veterans organization. But he was never a Nazi. He didn't treat me any differently from the others."

In contrast, the geography teacher, named Gessler, completely ignored my father. "He never called on me in class. I did not exist for him," he said, likening the behavior to similar treatment by the physical education instructor, Täubner, an avowed member of the Storm Troopers. "I saw him running around in a brown shirt and breeches, with black boots up to his knee. He was always punctual at class time and enthusiastically executed the Nazi greeting with his arm up and elbow locked in the prescribed way." But he consistently failed to allow my father to play soccer, leaving him on the bench.

Having put up with the daily bullying and harassment as the school's only Jewish student, my father, despite his desire to learn, was ready to quit the *Goetheschule*.

MY FATHER HAD ALWAYS LOOKED UP to his older brother Rudy, studious and serious from the earliest days. With his Mediterranean good looks, square jaw, raven hair, and dark eyes, his unique twelve-year-old presence is conspicuous in a class photograph from the 1924–25 school year.

Rudy had also attended the *Goetheschule* but was immediately drawn to study law. Sami and Helene were very supportive of his vocational pursuit.

"My parents sent him to the University of Heidelberg, where he spent two semesters studying pre-law. From there, he took a summer studying French in Clermont-Ferrant, deepening his knowledge of

French," my father recounted in his video interview. Rudy then transferred to the University of Munich, but when it was time to attend law school, he chose the University of Königsberg in East Prussia.

"My brother wanted to finish law school by getting practical experience in a law office after school hours," my father explained, noting that Uncle Georg agreed to have Rudy help at his law practice, which was increasingly engaged in defending people accused of specious political crimes.

On April 1, 1933, the Nazi-controlled government began a nationally coordinated harassment campaign against Germany's Jewish population. "My brother, then a university student and part-time law clerk to our uncle, was an eyewitness to the atrocities orchestrated by Otto Franck, the Nazi district leader of East Prussia. He did very well," my father added sarcastically, "because he earned his first stripes in anti-Jewish activities that would lead Hitler to later name him to lead the occupation government of Poland."

The coordinated anti-Jewish campaign also manifested itself in Ilmenau. As Rudy was witnessing anti-Semitic disturbances in Königsberg, Samuel Gronner opened the store on April 1 as usual, though there had been a public call for a show of force to intimidate Jewish shop owners with a three-day boycott of their businesses.

As a counter-measure, members of Ilmenau's Social Democratic Party and their supporters demonstrated their resistance by walking into the Wilhelm Sandler store, emerging with bags filled with newly purchased merchandise.

"For the occasion, my father wore his wartime insignia for service bravery in the Austrian Army, but this did not stop the Storm Troopers from forcibly entering our store, grabbing him and pushing him out with his regalia pinned to his lapel," said my father. "I don't remember the dirty language they had used to scrawl the graffiti on the sidewalk, but I vividly recall him kneeling down, medals and all, to whitewash it with a brush."

When the interviewer asked what his parents did after the incident, he said emphatically, "Nothing!" They had other things on their minds, namely Jochen's bar mitzvah a mere six weeks away.

As trucks and cars drove around Königsberg covered in anti-Semitic slogans, with tacit support from within the university community, Rudy, unlike his parents, became convinced that he had no future in Germany.

"I remember his long-distance phone call announcing he was leaving the country, with my mother shaken, crying and pleading that he stay in school to complete his degree," my father recalled. It turned out that Rudy's decision was supported by Uncle Georg, based on his own experience with the sudden shift in the legal establishment that cast aside the long-held principles of jurisprudence that had protected the democracy.

Sami and Helene pleaded with Rudy to come home and at least stay for the bar mitzvah, an event that would draw members of the family to Ilmenau.

Rudy arrived by train two days later, and my father accompanied his parents to the train station to meet his twenty-one year old sibling. Almost immediately, Jochen witnessed the arguments over what his parents thought was an impetuous decision.

Rudy reported seeing Jews being dragged into the streets, beaten with batons by brown-shirted Storm Troopers. "On the sidewalks they had scrawled slogans and defaced shop windows with all kinds of graffiti proclaiming the wickedness of the Jewish people and their treasonous faith to subvert the German Reich," my father said, quoting Rudy's account of what he had seen.

Rudy's eyewitness report described the arrest of a shopkeeper named Fischman, who was among a number of men pushed into a cart and hauled to the Gestapo headquarters in Königsberg. It was later learned, according to my father, "Herr Fischman, hands and feet tied, was put into a canvas bag that was attached to the express train to Danzig. He was dragged to death.

"Quite understandably, when you witness such atrocities at age twenty one, you get the shock of your life, and that's why, when he came home, he was adamant, saying, 'No more life here.'"

Rudy's vow to immediately leave for France was not as logistically involved as Uncle Georg's determination to wrap up his legal practice and household and move to Palestine. As an ardent Zionist, there was no other destination for the attorney Dr. Georg Sandler, his wife Meta, and three children—Rachel, Meir, and Daniel. Nonetheless, within the same interval beginning April 1, the five of them managed to be in Ilmenau and witness the bar mitzvah of Jochen Gronner on the Sabbath of May 13, 1933.

"My bar mitzvah was our last reunion with my maternal side of the family when we were all together alive," my father says in his videotaped interview.

The following Monday, Rudy boarded a train headed for Kehl, on the shores of the Rhine River, and subsequently walked across the bridge connecting to the city to Strasbourg, France. The same day, Georg and his family boarded a train to Munich, the first leg of the land and sea voyage to Palestine.

CHAPTER 6

Haifa

ONE MAY FORGIVE JOCHEN'S very busy working parents for not fully appreciating the gravity of his primary school complaints about bullying and harassment. He had been cared for at home all these years, they likely thought, and he is just going through an adjustment period to a new environment.

As my father explained in his videotaped interview decades later, they regarded it "as something normal."

While minimizing their younger son's complaints about the ribbing he received in school, Sami, Helene, and her brother Wilhelm were busily weighing their options in managing the growth of their enterprise for what they deemed the coming decades of prosperity. Even the expanded space they had leased in 1923 on Poststrasse was bursting at the seams.

The American fiscal rescue plan to settle Germany's post-war economic crisis began to take hold in the mid-1920s. My grandparents, likely with concurrence from Willi, head of the clan, concluded that the political stirrings on the far right and far left would subside. The decade had begun on a tentative footing, but Germany was positioned for a recovery, they reasoned.

And so, as my father reported, Sami had reached an agreement in 1927 to purchase the rectory on Ilmenau's main commercial street, 3 Moltkestrasse. A permit to erect a new ultramodern store at the site was granted on November 23, 1929—less than a month after the biggest collapse of the U.S. Stock Exchange set off the Great Depression.

Seemingly as part of a stealth marketing campaign to build interest in the forthcoming store, someone had briefed Ilmenau's *Die Henne* to publish the following item:

> *The newly constructed building on Moltkestrasse is visibly taking a step forward. As we hear it, the modern steel and concrete edifice will be completed in October. The three-story building will feature twelve show windows and two entrances. The basis for the entire interior furnishing design is both modern and yet practical, hence the new corner building will be an ornament gracing the streetscape.*

In his 1960s-era restitution claim to the East German authorities, my father provided further details of the new building. The ground floor housed departments for men's underwear, knitwear, and work clothes. The second level displayed women's and men's wear, with changing rooms alongside an area featuring full-service tailoring and alteration services.

The seven-room family quarters, with a private side entrance and stairwell, occupied the space above the sales floors. An additional attic level below the flat roof housed a three-room apartment for a caretaker, including laundry and storage space.

"The store's interior design was of solid oak showcases," my father wrote. "Men's accessories were arranged in custom designed drawers."

On December 3, 1929, *Die Henne* published a glowing account of the grand opening:

> The opening of the Wilhelm Sandler department store was a business event of a special kind, attracting wide public participation. The city administration and city council were also represented. Unreserved recognition was given for the enterprising, foresighted mercantile spirit, which had found its creative impulse in this exemplary work. With this new magnificent department store, the company created for our city an example of entrepreneurial enjoyment, through which Ilmenau has taken steps to be among the forward-thinking cities of Thuringia.

The ultramodern Wilhelm Sandler building thus was elevated in status among the three major Jewish-owned retail stores—including the popular Eichnbronner department store featuring its "White Weeks" sales of chic Parisian fashions, and the Berliner Warenhaus, whose owners Nussbaum and Gabbe (both named Max) regularly touted their "99-Pfennig-Tagen" sales days.[11]

Those heady days, filled with optimism and great enthusiasm for the future, turned out to be short-lived. Just as their younger son was entering the *Goetheschule*, the Gronners were still hopeful that the newly elected Nazi government in Thuringia was merely a nuisance that would pass.

Yet by the time of Jochen's bar mitzvah in 1933, and Rudy's and Georg's decisions to emigrate, they maintained stoic pride until Jochen's school fights were no longer tolerable.

In 1935, they worked out a plan for him to spend his summer vacation with Rudy, who had by then settled in Paris. Since Jochen had been studying French, Sami and Helene thought the time spent in Paris would help him advance his language skills. "I am thankful for that opportunity," my father recalled.

When Rudy had first crossed into Strasbourg, he had found work as an unskilled laborer in a weaving plant. Shortly thereafter he made his way to Paris, where he found a job working in a cleaning store. In the interim, as my father explained, "Somehow my father managed to send some money across the border into Switzerland, where he opened an account in the Schweitzer Kantonalbank in Basel. By 1934, Rudy was able to withdraw some of those funds to buy a cleaning store of his own from a Frenchman."

Paris was teeming with Jewish refugees from Germany when Jochen arrived by train for his summer visit. "My parents had wanted me to experience life without the protection of home, and I am thankful for that too, because I got to see a lot of misery in my young years.

"My brother took me several times to refugee centers near the Place de la République, where refugees congregated and lived on handouts. Among them were writers, poets, painters, doctors, and political functionaries who had formerly belonged to Germany's leftist parties. Some prominently displayed the insignia of the Reichsbanner Front, the anti-Fascist movement. I remember this vividly. They were all very depressed, very much distraught, and dressed in rags."

Following his summer in Paris, Jochen returned to Ilmenau to begin studies at the town's technical school in preparation for a career in mechanical engineering. Though Germany was now governed by an anti-Semitic regime headed by Adolf Hitler, my father had no problems crossing the border and returning home.

He attended classes in the afternoon so that he could gain hands-on experience in a local machine shop, a prerequisite for an engineering degree. But other plans were afoot. At the behest of Sami and Helene, their close friend and committed Zionist Max Gabbe, the co-owner of the Berliner Warenhaus, had set in motion the bureaucratic process of applying for an exit visa for Jochen, so he could continue his schooling in Palestine.

"I presume this was Mother's doing," my father observed, noting, "having come from a religious home, and being very Jewish minded, this was very natural." Another likely reason may have been her younger brother Georg's decision to leave Germany with his family, and that Jochen would have family support in Palestine.

The following May, the paperwork was completed and Jochen traveled to Berlin. "Bet Halutz was a transitional home where young Jewish people gathered to organize, and learn Hebrew and modern Jewish history, in preparation for their emigration to Palestine," my father explained.

The Summer Olympics of 1936 garnered worldwide attention when Jesse Owens, the black American track and field star, captured four gold medals, including one for the long-jump record that held for the next quarter century. Two months later Jochen again left Ilmenau for Niederschönhausen, just south of Berlin, as part of the World Zionist Organization aliyah program to bring young Jews to Palestine. Each prospective emigrant went through a career orientation, and because of his apprenticeship, Jochen was selected for the metalworking shop.

"After four weeks, I was chosen as a representative of the group to help determine the qualification of candidates for emigration. There were sixty boys and girls, but only forty could be selected," my father recalled, noting that Britain, which took charge of Ottoman-controlled Palestine after the First World War, had issued a so-called "Command

Paper of 1922" imposing limitations on Jewish immigration, so "that the immigrants should not be a burden upon the people of Palestine as a whole, and that they should not deprive any section of the present population of their employment."[12]

"I was eliminated from consideration right away because I was too old, compared to the others," he explained. But his opportunity came the following month, when a new group of forty-four youngsters was assembled from among those who were selected to attend the Technion, the technical university in Haifa. The group sailed together on an Italian steamship, arriving on Monday, January 25, 1937.

As the ship docked in the Haifa harbor, he likely saw the golden dome of the Bahá'í Temple, a landmark I would contemplate some two decades later upon my family's departure from Israel, by then the restored national home for the Jewish diaspora.

NOT HAVING HEARD FROM JOCHEN about his voyage for a month, Sami and Helene penned a frantic letter dated February 22 and addressed to their nephews, Siegfried and Heinz Grünspan, the sons of Helene's sister Paula who had already left Germany and settled in Tel Aviv.

Sami's note was typically less emotional than his wife's:

> We have just received your airmail letter and we were pleased to hear that you are healthy and that all is well with both of you. Health wise, we are, thank God, fine, but let's keep quiet about everything else, since your situation there is always better than ours.
>
> . . . On January 18 I drove to the border with Jochen, where he took off two days later from Trieste. The farewell was a bit difficult. But let's hope that everything is for the better. Staying here and being hounded made it impossible

for him to learn anything. If you think of everything else, it is an infinitely bitter lot. God be with him and you.

Jochen is at the Technikum in Haifa. His address is Haifa-Geulah Beth Katz—Chevrat Noar Germanith. We are surprised that you do not know his return address, which he had shared when he sent a card to Onkel Georg around February 2. Additionally Anny Gattil had written to her sister that she visited you, and that you had spoken about Jochen and his visit with Anny in Haifa. We would like to hear about it in detail. Does Onkel Georg have no interest in Jochen? His behavior seems to us very peculiar.

We acknowledge that he is very busy. Yet I think you have to set aside a short time for this. Jochen is well cared for, as we have already heard from a friend, who made the effort and took time to find out about his exact accommodation and whereabouts. This person, who serves in the police in Afula, wrote us a very lovely and long letter, and he is happy to be of help. We have not yet been briefed on the nature and duration of the studies—but we hope to be informed soon. We are concerned about the many things that Jochen had brought with him, and hope he takes care of them and maybe gives you some things for safekeeping. Most importantly, he should care that his laundry is not ruined. Let's please hear from you soon again. Farewell, most heartfelt greetings from

your Uncle Sami

My grandmother's note, sent in the same letter, did not hold back her emotional distress:

My very dear ones!

Your last letter gave us a lot of joy because I can now infer that you are in good health, and that you are professionally satisfied. I feel very disappointed that you still had not had a chance to meet Jochen. Yet even more pained as I have entirely relied on you and Uncle Georg and Aunt Meta! I do not hold any grudge that not one of you was there to meet him at the port. But since I did put this in writing, I would have expected that one of his relatives would at least come say hello to the child in a foreign country! I don't know if Jochen feels that way, but for me, as a mother, it was sickening!

I am most disappointed by Georg and Meta, who have children of their own and who could best sympathize with how I came to rely on them out of great concern for my child! Granted, they are preoccupied and have their own worries, yet it would still be possible to write a short response to my letter!

I have tussled in my mind whether I might have let some ill will come toward them, because I simply cannot explain or believe this behavior!

Well-in any case, I had a better fortune! How a young friend of ours, in contrast, has behaved cannot be described! His care of Jochen's needs was truly maternal, and with what length and detail he had provided us with reports! He is really a very impressive person I will never forget! Via Any Gattel I've also heard indirectly about Jochen and you must also have heard, because you've met him. I hope to hear from you more often in the future.

May you both and all of your loved ones be greeted heartily from aunt Lenchen

CHAPTER 7

Planning an Exit

I n the letter to his nephews, Sami's comment to "let's keep quiet about everything else" was an oblique reference to the increasingly worsening situation in Nazi Germany. Josef Goebbels, Hitler's propagandist, was obsessed by the economic success experienced by the relatively small number of German Jews who, in 1933, accounted for less than one percent of the entire the population.[13]

Yet the Nazi Party's official organ, *Der Stürmer*, ceaselessly fanned flames of hate against Germany's Jewish population with a barrage of anti-Semitic tropes blaming them for all the nation's ills.

Ilmenau was not immune from the propaganda campaign. It intensified after Jochen's departure, as the town was flooded with fliers with bold headlines: "Buy Only from Germans," and "Whoever Buys From Jews Is a National Traitor," calling for a boycott of all Jewish enterprises.

Set in agate type, the entire left column of the page recited an interminable précis of the Nazi ideology that Adolf Hitler had spelled out in *Mein Kampf*, laden with his view of history as an incessant struggle among races and the need to preserve the purity of the German nation.

Atop the right hand column ran a bold-faced sub-headline, "Who Is a Jew? What is a Jewish Enterprise?"

The text could not be more blatant—dumbed down for Goebbels' intended mass audience:

> In the future, there should no longer be any doubts as to whether the individual is in front of a Jew. Just as we naturally expect that the Jewish racial member will do the same in the first place [with respect] to his blood and faith-comrades, so we expect national principles that the German national comrade goes to his German national comrades.
>
> Therefore, show that you are German and act German, then you perform your duty.

As an ominous warning the text included a sub-heading "Jews—Look at each other!" followed by a list of the individual names of Ilmenau's Jewish residents, their addresses, the maiden names of their spouses, and their respective businesses or professions. Among the thirty-seven names and seven firms listed were Samuel and Helene Gronner, née Sandler, and the firm Wilhelm Sandler, repeating the names of the owners.

"The Jews are our misfortune!" the missive trumpeted as a closing takeaway message.

Unlike the prior call for boycott in 1933, when many of my grandparents' friends and neighbors defied the Nazis, there now was a pall of fear in the once-friendly town as Gestapo agents monitored who among the residents dared resist the national duty to shun Jewish-owned establishments. Non-compliance risked social ostracism and even physical intimidation, as neighbors increasingly reported to the police who was seen emerging from the Jewish-owned shops, including the prominent Wilhelm Sandler clothing store.

Over the subsequent year, sales steadily plummeted, and Sami and Helene had trouble keeping up with their expenses. After Jochen had left for Palestine, the declining business revenue, and my grandparents' growing inability to support the debts incurred from new building construction, were taking a toll on their well-being. No one was there to witness the arguments about what to do next, but I can imagine that Helene insisted that they plan to leave Germany. The business has no future, she likely argued, and thank God our boys are in a better place. The Sandler kin were dispersing. Siegfried Grünspan had emigrated to Palestine at age twenty-seven in 1933 just as Georg had done with his wife and children. Paula passed away on April 2, 1935, and Heinz, her younger son, left for Palestine that August.

Her niece Recha was married in January 1938 to Richard Cohn and moved to his home town Halle after a brief honeymoon in Palestine. The couple was expecting their first child in the fall and hoping to emigrate. In Helene's mind, it was only a matter of time before the widowed Bernhard would leave Germany as well.

It's possible that Sami finally relented to her pleadings and agreed to make an exploratory trip to Palestine to determine the suitability of emigration for him and his wife. He convinced Rudy to join him in reuniting in Palestine with Jochen, Georg's family and the Grünspan brothers.

I found it odd that, despite what must have been a busy schedule, Sami and his sons had taken the time to pose for a professional photo I found in my father's collection. Why go through the trouble and expense of such a memento if your intent is to come back, I wonder?

Perhaps Sami knew this would be his last chance to be with his sons in person. The back of the black and white photo bears a handwritten inscription: *In remembrance of our beautiful get-together in Erez Israel, March 16, 1938.*

JUST DAYS EARLIER, THE CONFIDENT WEHRMACHT had marched into Austria with virtually no resistance to declare the *Anschluss,* a unification of the two German-speaking nations into a reconstituted Reich. "Those of the same blood belong in the same Reich," Hitler had declared to win the support of the German-speaking majority of Austrians.

This event was no doubt disconcerting to Sami. Though he was with his beloved sons away from the turmoil, he feared for his parents and siblings, who had made a comfortable life in Vienna since migrating from Silesia some two decades earlier. As he knew from personal experience, they too would now be exposed to the effects of Hitler's anti-Semitic venom.

Official government-instituted anti-Semitism in Germany was rooted in a series of national civic laws, adopted by the Reichstag in 1935, implementing Hitler's racist ideology. These so-called "Nuremberg Laws" institutionalized many of the racial theories underpinning Nazi ideology and provided the legal framework for the systematic persecution of Jews in Germany.[14]

The *Anschluss* emboldened the Nazi dictatorship to escalate its persecution of Jews to protect what they referred to as Germany's indigenous and superior "Aryan race."

In *Life in the Third Reich*, historian William Carr of Sheffield University, reports:

> *As the German economy moved into top gear, the big industrial concerns, eager to take over their Jewish competitors at knock-down prices, pressed the*

government to proceed to the 'Aryanization' of the economy. . . Following the
Anschluss with Austria, [Hermann] Göring issued a decree ordering Jews to
register all property above five thousand Marks in value and forbidding them
to sell it without permission . . . In the summer of 1938 Jewish doctors, dentists,
and lawyers were forbidden to offer their services to Aryans.[15]

My grandparents—most likely Helene, eager to emigrate—thought that the government's edict to transfer ownership of their business would provide a means to recoup their investment in order to finance their planned emigration from Germany. By then, Sami had determined from his trip to Palestine that his wife would be unable to withstand the notorious Middle Eastern heat waves. Nonetheless, irrespective of their eventual destination—be it the Western Hemisphere or other temperate regions—the immediate objective was therefore, in American parlance, to take the money and run.

It soon became evident that they were underestimating the intention of the Nazi strategy—namely, to orchestrate a nationwide boycott intended to suck the blood and sweat that Jews had sacrificed in building their business assets.

In making his case for restitution by the East German authorities years later, my father referred to "the well-known shenanigans" of the boycotts to drive profitable businesses like his parents' into inevitable worthless decay.

Among the papers in the stack he had left me were critical documents related to the forced "sale" of the Wilhelm Sandler store in Ilmenau to a non-Jewish shopkeeper named Hilmar Näder. The back-and-forth correspondence among the involved parties illustrates the charade that was being played out, as if this were a normal business transaction.

A copy of a hand-written document on Wilhelm Sandler stationery, and dated July 22, 1938, presents my grandfather's outline, in general terms, of what he considered a reasonable valuation of the Sandler firm for transfer to Herr Näder.

"I confirm receipt of 1,000 RM (one thousand) from Herrn Hilmar Näder, presently living in Gräfenroda, as deposit toward the purchase of property at 3 Moltkestrasse in Ilmenau for 140,000 (one hundred and forty thousand) Reichsmark," my grandfather wrote in a distinctive Sütterlin script.

(Thankfully, my friend Rainer enlisted Ilmenau's archivist, Frau Arnold, to decipher what to contemporary readers appears like pen strokes aligned in a series of pointed mountain peaks, interspersed with doodles of vertical curves and lines that extend above and below the horizontal plane of text. Once taught in schools and commonly used, this cursive style had fallen into disuse by the mid-twentieth century.)

As if he had some negotiation leverage, my grandfather stipulated that the exact amount of inventory and furnishings would be settled prior to contract closing, at which time Mr. Näder would produce the balance in cash, although evidence of his ability to pay that sum was required by August 30. (Samuel picked September 15 as the date for closing—unaware that this would be the birth date of his first grandchild and namesake nine years later.)

As is often the case in such negotiations, a meticulously detailed "First Draft" was prepared by an attorney, Erich Reinmann. In the preamble, he states he is personally acquainted with the seller, and attests that he has proof of the buyer's Aryan status, having a membership card of the buyer with a photo ID and Nazi Party membership number 606650.

A stipulation for consummating the deal was Mr. Näder's obligation to provide proof that he had secured the necessary funds to pay the purchase price.

The document lists the property purchase price at 141,750 RM, from which Herr Näder was obliged to transfer 13,500 RM to the account of the Thuringia District (Gau), netting my grandparents a theoretical 128,250 RM. Other terms covered Herr Näder's assumption of a mortgage with Landes-Hyptekebank in Weimar in consideration of his payment of the net purchase price for the property.

From that amount, the agreement stipulates my grandfather would pay the cost to remove liens on the property held by the Thuringian Landesbank, the construction firm Rudolf Glaser, as well as security bond from the insurance firm Roos & Cahn in Bielefeld. By my calculation, the deductions whittled down the cash he was left with to 61,250 RM.

But even this was too much for the local economic counselor in Thuringia. Ignoring the officially sanctioned boycott of Jewish-owned enterprises, the Thuringian district of the Nazi party sent the following to Herr Näder:

> Re: Aryanization of Wilhelm Sandler enterprise, Ilmenau.
>
> From of the draft agreement received today I see that the property Ilmenau, Moltkestrasse 3, owned by the non-Aryan Gronner, shall change into your hands for a price of 140,000 Reichsmark (onehundred and forty thousand). However, the last assessed tax value is only 110,000 Reichsmark. At aryanizations, normally the last assessed value is the valid base. For that reason, I ask you to initiate a new proceeding on this base. I remark, that 10% of the total value are to be paid to the Gau (District) Thüringen.
>
> I ask that you consider this point during your negotiations and to make it part of the contract.

I note that this order will be made not only against you, but against every potential buyer.

The letter, emblazoned with the swastika letterhead of the National Socialist Workers Party, closed with "Heil Hitler".

In helping me translate this correspondence, my friend Rainer did not mince words, explaining: "It's a 'hint' by the Nazi business consultant to Näder to pressure your grandfather to sell the property at a price even lower than agreed, because the alleged 'last assessed value' was lower. It's one of those typical Nazi phrases with which they tried to provide pseudo-legitimization and the appearance of normal governmental conduct to their greed."

When it came to the negotiation about the value of store, another missive was addressed to Herr Näder, also signed "Heil Hitler":

After receiving information fixing the value of the warehouse of Sandler (Samuel Gronner, Ilmenau,) I serve notice that under no circumstances can I recognize a value of about 60,000RM. The balance sheet of Samuel Gronner on 31 December 1937 reports an inventory of 37,589RM. Since the Sandler firm reported a comparable value in 1935, it is inexplicable to me how it is possible that in that interval an unrecognized reserve of 23,000RM could be set aside.

I would ask you to point out to Mr. Gronner in your negotiations that the value of the warehouse shown as hidden profits in comparison to its balance sheet cannot be recognized. I reserve the right to require the tax office in Ilmenau to carry out an additional audit if Mr. Gronner does not waive his claim in this amount. I consider accepting the value of the warehouse at the most 45- to 48,000RM in relation to its balance sheet of 31 December 1937.

The indignities visited upon my grandparents were entirely glossed over by the back and forth business correspondence. Even as Herr Näder reported that he had secured funding for his purchase, as he was obligated to do, his very civil, business-like letter addressed my grandfather as "Dear Mr. Gronner" and signed off "Sincerely!" with exclamation.

The chicanery of the Nazis makes it hard to determine the absolute final amount of money my grandparents actually were able to collect for the business they had built over some three decades. Records note that the handover occurred on September 24, 1938.

In his 1960s affidavit to the East German authorities, my father referred to a written statement from Reimann, the attorney, who had set up the sales contract: "[He] told me that the contract was subject to conditions that were inhuman even by his own sense of justice, and how these infuriated him. I emphasize that Mr. Reinmann, to the best of our knowledge, had been an active member of the German National People's Party." (The *Deutschnationale Volkspartei* or DNVP, for a time was a Nazi coalition partner in the Bundestag.)

Although the business was now in the hands of Herr Näder, Sami and Helene were allowed to remain as tenants in the expansive apartment they had built atop the two levels of showrooms. The sales contract stipulated that they would pay Herr Näder up to 30RM monthly toward rent for him to live elsewhere in town, but that they would need to vacate no later than January 2, 1940.

Sami and Helene thought this would be sufficient time to plan their departure.

It was not to be.

CHAPTER 8

Outbreak of War

I N THE DARKNESS OF THE GALILEAN HILLS, Jochen strained his eyes to spot any slight movement that would signal a potential incursion. Within a week of his arrival in Haifa, he had signed up to volunteer after school hours for guard duty at disparate locations that the Zionist military leaders had determined required defensive positions; they were preparing for the inevitable confrontation with the Arab clans who had lived in the region for generations and felt threatened by the growing numbers of European Jewish settlers.

My father's arrival coincided with the latest round of periodic revolts by Arabs against the British Mandate—this latest one had begun in 1936. Arab rebellions had been instigated since the 1920s by a rabidly anti-Zionist and fiery cleric, Haj Amin al Husseini, the Mufti of Jerusalem. Haj Amin's tactic of nocturnal raids against the Jewish outposts and established settlements was designed to instill fear and thereby prevent the arrival of more Jewish refugees in Palestine. His efforts did not dissuade many financially strapped peasants and absentee Arab landowners who had acquired property during the Ottoman era from selling land at appreciated value for Jewish settlement. [16]

"Little did I know that this meant I would be indoctrinated and recruited by the clandestine Haganah organization," my father recalled decades later, referring to his assent for guard duty. He called this "the beginning of my national service in Palestine."

Though only in his teens, Jochen experienced a baptism by fire of sorts in paramilitary activity. He spent his days in class at the Technion, but on many evenings he underwent training or was taken to outposts to defend newly built defensive positions.

"My commander also turned out to also be one of my teachers. At that time, there still was cooperation between the Mandatory government and the Haganah. Rifles were issued to the Haifa fire brigade along with fire fighter caps." With his typical British elocution of military terminology, he added, "Others joined the Third Staffordshire battalion, billeted at the time in Allenby barracks in Bat Galim, Haifa, where they were armed and trained to participate in actions against rebelling Arabs."

The network of fortified settlements was the brainchild of Avraham Harzfeld, a pioneer Zionist who had escaped Tsarist imprisonment in Siberia in 1914. His "Tower and Stockade" concept was to build fortifications virtually overnight. Among these was Tel Amal, begun in December 1936. My father was also dispatched to a similar installation, which eventually became Kibbutz Hanita in the Western Galilee.

With cooperation of the Mandatory authorities, some Haganah volunteers were armed as auxiliary police, later gaining official status as Jewish Settlement Police, armed with rifles, Lewis machine guns, mortars and hand grenades. As a paramilitary force, the Haganah coordinated defense by using the lights atop the watchtowers to communicate with the regional command posts, my father explained.

Referring to his role during that period, he recalled his initial encounters with contemporaries who eventually became Israel's national leaders—Yitzhak Rabin, Yigal Allon, and Moshe Dayan.

Britain was well aware that German Jews like my father and his family were eager to emigrate to Palestine to escape the effects of organized state anti-Semitism in Germany, and this likely provided them with a reason to help new arrivals defend themselves.

But Haj Amin's open calls for rebellion against the Empire and promotion of sabotage to instill fear to curtail the influx of Jews from Europe left Britain in a no-win predicament. With one eye on the growing threat of a Fascist Germany, Britain also had to contend with an internecine conflict in Palestine. In 1937, Herbert Samuel, the British High Commissioner, ordered the arrest of the Arab Council leadership, causing Haj Amin to flee across the Jordan to the so-called Trans-Jordan territory that Britain had ceded to the Hashemite royal family headed by King Abdullah.

Britain's efforts to appear even-handed led to a special commission and hearings in London and in Jerusalem where an Amin relative excoriated the authorities for allowing continued settlement by Jews from Europe. Ignoring the historical fact of Jewish presence since Biblical days, and the peaceful coexistence between Jews and Arabs for centuries, Amin claimed Britain was conspiring with Jews to change what he termed was the Arab character of Palestine.

The Peel Commission subsequently issued a decree ordering an immediate cessation of Jewish immigration and sale of land for their resettlement.

"Our reaction to this was obvious," my father explained, noting spontaneous uprisings in the major Jewish population centers like Tel Aviv, Haifa, and Jerusalem. "Government buildings—including the courts—were pelted with bottles, stones and firebombs," he said to describe how the *Yishuv*—the Hebrew term used for the collective Jewish settlement—vented its anger against Britain.

The British military continued to support the Haganah self-defense of the Jewish settlements, but the authorities instituted a blockade to bar further immigrants from entering. Still, clandestine efforts to smuggle desperate refugees were coordinated by Zionist organizations abroad and by the Jewish Agency for Palestine.

THROUGH HIS INVOLVEMENT WITH THE HAGANAH, and the influence of socialist Zionist ideas from mentors like Harzfeld, the young Jochen came to adopt notions of communal, worker-oriented idealism. His social circle encompassed members of *Hashomer Hatzair*, a Zionist youth movement that promoted settlement in Eretz Israel and building a utopian, worker-based society distinctly different from that of traditional European Jewry. In the trove of memorabilia my father left me are many black-and-white snapshots of him in the company of young men and women at various social events, hikes in the hills of Galilee, and other outdoor activities.

The photos do not disclose what was on these young peoples' minds. But imagine being unencumbered teens and idealistic young adults on their own, aspiring to build a new nation, free of parental supervision, accountable only to themselves, and you sense the liberating feeling they must have experienced.

Uprooted from their native European homes, and participating in the founding of a reconstituted Jewish national homeland, these young people rightly took their place as *bona fide* members of what Tom Brokaw came to coin "The Greatest Generation."

My father's hectic schedule left precious little time to sit down and write letters home, and it frustrated his mother to no end. On numerous occasions she complained in letters to her family about this lack of correspondence.

Toward the end of summer 1939, a letter from Rudy arrived, presumably in Haifa; he was reporting that he had been drafted into the French army. As a non-citizen, Rudy was given the choice to join the French Foreign Legion, and in writing the letter, he wanted Jochen to know that all his worldly goods would go to his kid brother should he not survive. Days later, on September 1, Germany attacked Poland, drawing an immediate British and French response as the Allies declared war.

"This was the first and only communication I had from my brother until the armistice with France," my father recalls in his Shoah Foundation video testimony, referring to the Vichy administration, the puppet regime that collaborated with Nazi Germany, beginning in July 1940.

In Germany, things went from bad to worse.

On the night of November 9, 1938, hooligans throughout Germany undertook a well-coordinated rampage against Jewish-owned homes, businesses, along with religious and cultural institutions. In Thuringia nine synagogues were attacked and at least two sanctuaries were plundered and their contents set ablaze.

As my grandparents had already discovered, Thuringia had led the way toward the *de facto* expropriation of Jewish property when Fritz Sauckel, the district Nazi leader, established a bureaucratic process within the regional economic development department for the takeover of Jewish-owned property under Göring's "aryanization" decree.[17]

Locally, the regional Nazi propaganda tool, *Thüringer Gauzeitung*, called in early October for continued united action against Jews, to be completed by mid-1939 at the latest. On November 17, the message was reinforced: "Do Not Soften Up!" its headline screamed.

In order to intentionally provide illusory evidence that the civic unrest resulted from spontaneous grass-roots combustion, the official word had come down to local police from the highest echelons not to interfere with the gangs. There was conscious separation between the Nazi machinery and government prosecution, with orders not to interfere in police matters.[18]

It was not until after the fact that Theodore Klinkhardt, of the Eisenach state's attorney office, reported on his personal inspection to get a first-hand look at the effect of the vandalism: In one case, he wrote, "the entire contents of four rooms, kitchen and dining room were disturbed. Nothing was untouched. Furniture was toppled and smashed. Porcelain, glass and crystal shattered on the floor. Pictures torn from walls and smashed. The entire contents of one room were a heap of rubble. Only the bedroom of the couple was undamaged."[19]

A state investigator named Ebock, assigned to Ilmenau, reported on November 10 to the state attorney general's office in Gotha that there had been an afternoon "demonstration" by students and faculty of the local finance school. "Six Jewish males arrested, six turned over to police, two taken to Buchenwald, four released."[20] Samuel Gronner was detained in Buchenwald for one month under "protective custody."

The nationwide pogrom against Germany's Jewish population prompted Britain's organized Jewish community to persuade British authorities to mount two operations to save Germany's Jews. The first, well known as the *Kindertransport*, enabled distraught German parents to entrust some ten thousand unaccompanied children to caretakers for safe travel to Britain. A lesser-known mission was aimed at adult Jewish men who had been caught up in the November pogrom.

Richard Cohn, an attorney and husband of my grandparents' niece Recha, was among the fortunate four thousand Jewish men, both married and single, who managed to be included in the transports from Berlin and Vienna, arriving at a former military base, Camp Kitchener, in the summer of 1939.

The objective of the mission was to enable family members to come to Britain, especially wives who could obtain so-called "domestic service visas" for travel to Britain.[21] It was no doubt traumatic for Richard, safe in Britain, to await approval for his young wife Recha and their daughter Hanneli, born days after the November *Reichspogrom*, to be granted an exit permit. Her father Bernhard had by then departed for Palestine, arriving in April 1939 to the delight of his sons Heinz and Siegfried.

THE OUTBREAK OF WAR IN SEPTEMBER spelled a dire future for Germany's Jews. In her living quarters above what had been the family store, my grandmother brooded over the tragic fate of the landmark family enterprise. Since 1907, expanding through multiple locations on Poststrasse, and for the past decade housed in its ultramodern edifice on Moltkestrasse 3, the enterprise had borne the name of its founder—her brother Wilhelm Sandler. Now, coming home from her daily errands, she could not bear seeing, high above the rounded upper corner, the garish letters that spelled out the name of its new owner—the Nazi Näder—to whom her husband had been forced to relinquish the family business.

By the end of the year, Sami and Helene were contractually obliged to vacate the apartment as well, and the only place where they were allowed to live was a house designated exclusively for Jews.

Their letters to Jerusalem were appropriately guarded:

January 14, 1940

  My dear Bernhard!

  I often think of you, very often! Your upcoming birthday prompted me to give visible expression to this idea, although I'm not 100% convinced that these lines will reach you. In any case, I wish you all the best in the new year of life, fulfillment of your own wishes.

  Anyway, you have all the reasons to be satisfied with your good fortune, even though some wishes might be not be realized. If only they could bring Recha and the child together with Richard, then you will, I imagine, be fully satisfied! But you can rely on Recha! She is very brave, and will always be in difficult situations. Incidentally, Hanneli is a very sweet creature.

  It is sad that the father and grandfather can not observe her development. Our housemate, the dear Willi, left us yesterday. He went into a nursing home in Frankfurt (am Main). Now it is even more lonely for us! Since the middle of last month we have been living in Goethestr. 11 in a miniature apartment. My husband expects a speedy emigration. (Not I!). Through Recha I hear from time to time about you. But it's been weeks since receiving notice about our children. God help them! For you and your children I am wishing all the best, and greet you and them heartily,

  Your Lenchen

Dear Bernhard and Heinz!

  It has been long—quite long—not having directly heard from one another. The urge and the craving for a written expression of this emotional distress loom ever more large.

  You must have heard by now of our misfortune in Berlin last September 12. We had been summoned for the purpose of visa issuance, and the day before a general lock-down was declared, although this should be of short duration. We are now fretfully awaiting the time.

Despite his ability to keep us informed, we have no news from Jochen since October 24. We are quite concerned about his life, his coming and goings. Also don't know whether any of the relatives are looking after the boy. From Rudy, who is interned, we last had news on December 11. Recha and the child were with us, but we are usually in contact with Halle. Now we have to work.

We have taken note of your expansion, and happily wish you, dear Bernhard, on the occasion of your birthday, health and strength so that you can derive satisfaction and joy working in the midst of your children. From the heart I wish you peace of mind.

My brother Salo from Breslau who went to Manila (Philippines) and continued on to Shanghai, has recently landed in New York. That can tell you something about his emigration, which is so rich in experiences.

Today I wish you all the best. Remain warmly greeted by your brother and uncle

Sami

PALESTINE WAS NOT SPARED from the growing international confrontation between the Axis and Allied powers. After all, it was under control of the British Mandatory government. But here Britain had to deal with a uniquely local problem. With English forces deployed in Europe, and confronting Italian and German campaigns in North Africa, Britain could scarcely afford the distraction of the Arab-Jewish conflict in Palestine.

The various factions represented within the Jewish Agency began their own internal debate about the quandary they faced. As my father wrote: "On the one hand they needed to help the Allies, specifically the British Empire; but to fight the Nazis, on the other hand, they had to fight the implementation of the White Paper." In fact, in 1939 Britain revised the 1922 document by imposing a rigid annual quota of 10,000

Jewish immigrants. David Ben-Gurion, the head of the Jewish Agency, proposed a two-pronged strategy—opposing Britain's immigration ban while helping Britain and the Allies.

That is how they came to train young immigrants for underground activities in the occupied parts of Europe, while calling on others to volunteer for Palestinian units of the British armed forces. Some 30,000 Jews from around the world had fought for Britain throughout the second world war.[22]

As the Technion staff and student body were pulled unto a wartime footing, the pursuit of education was essentially curtailed. Jochen left school and moved to Jerusalem to help Bernhard in his new Café Atara, at the very beginning of its reputation as a haunt for the many displaced intellectuals, writers, and journalists who had fled Germany. It was also a hub for the many Jerusalem-based correspondents of foreign media covering the Middle East wartime theater.

Rudy's prior letters to Jochen, in care of Bernhard in Jerusalem, had borne return addresses from occupied France, but this changed after July. "Shortly thereafter," my father later said, "the return address of his next letter was Bou'rfa, Morocco, in which he describes that he is in a labor camp with four and half thousand 'co-religionists.' He tells me he is well and asks me to respond."

By August 1940, the twenty-year-old Jochen volunteered for the British army, which, on the basis of his background as an experienced machinist, assigned him to the Royal Engineers—the English counterpart to the U.S. Army Corps of Engineers.

Because of his military status, the only means of communication with his family was through the International Red Cross. "At least I had a sign that someone in my immediate family was alive," he said. "I did not know about the fate of my parents at that time because even my brother could only tell me that Father and Mother had to leave; no one knew the circumstances at the time."

Rudy related that, among the many Jews he encountered in Morocco, he ran into Uncle Siegfried, the last-born brother of Samuel Gronner, who had by then adopted a Francophone version of his name, Sylvain. Cognizant that all correspondence from the labor camp was subject to censorship, Rudy wrote only, "Uncle Sylvain will probably be out of here next month."

CHAPTER 9

War, Love, and Death

W E WERE DISPATCHED TO THE SUEZ CANAL zone and received our basic training as well as combat advanced training in chemical warfare, demolition and night combat," my father recalled decades later.

In the summer of 1942, prior to the attack against Rommel's Panzer Division at El-Alamein, he had been part of an advanced stage company tasked with camouflaging aircraft, heavy guns, and anti-aircraft embankments. He recalled:

> My unit was stationed six miles east of El-Alamein. On September 13, all hell broke loose with the opening of heavy artillery fire against the German lines. Five days later I was called to the commanding officer's office, where I met some officers of the intelligence branch of the Military Police. They told me that I had been selected to accompany a group of German POWs to the prisoner camp in the Canal Zone. I was not to speak or make any gestures as if I understand German. I was to take mental notes and be debriefed each evening. Due to the wartime conditions, the transport would last four days.

When his special assignment ended, Jochen had a struggle reuniting with his unit because of the Allied advance, but he eventually joined them in Sollum, near the Libyan border. Not much later, he began an important phase of his British military experience that would serve him well in his next role in postwar Palestine.

> *I was selected to attend training courses at the Tel-el-Kebir Ordnance base. There I learned to repair the barrels of heavy guns as well as their heat treatment. Much later, this turned out to be a tremendous asset to the fledgling Israeli army. Quite a number of my comrades who were posted in all-Jewish units in the same general area were directly involved in picking up booty from the retreating Afrika Korps and their fascist Black Shirts support units. Some of this booty was smuggled back to Palestine and ended up in the arms caches of the Haganah.*

Jochen received no news from his parents as he resolved to join the British armed forces and do what he could to defeat the Nazis. What is clear, however, is that while they were forced to remain in their cramped quarters at 11 Goethestrasse in Ilmenau, they were in financial straits even after disposing of their property in September 1939.

In his 1960s restitution claim to the East German authorities, my father stated:

> *It is clear to us today that our father cashed out his life insurance policies from Allianz and Stuttgarter a mere four months after this date (even though they had been declared premium-free) and that he never came into possession of the full amount granted to him by the Nazis. He had to vacate the flat and sell the furniture at a bargain price in order to support himself and our mother. The latter clearly proves the Jewish tax imposed on our father was offset by the*

balance still due to him from the sale of the business and land. In addition, there are the gold and silver items from private property delivered by our father, for which he was not compensated.

Now, two years into the war, living in abject poverty, having been cheated out of virtually all their assets, my grandmother had to endure the most devastating setback when her husband was arrested by the Gestapo on November 28, 1941, and hauled to Buchenwald one more time.

The ostensible reason, which I eventually saw on his official "rap sheet" in the German archives, was that the Jew "was overheard discussing the war with a Polish person." While there's no proof, this arrest could have been retribution instigated by Fritz Sauckel to punish the one Jew in Ilmenau who had dared slap the Nazi agitator in front of his store a decade earlier. Within months, Sauckel's hatred of Jews would merit promotion to Plenipotentiary-General for Labor Mobilization—essentially the national head of slave labor mobilization.[23]

For his crime against the Reich, the fifty-six-year-old Samuel Gronner was assigned to hard labor in the camp's gravel pit.

MEANWHILE, AFTER THE ESTABLISHMENT of the Nazi-puppet government in Vichy, France, Sami's brother, now calling himself Sylvain, was released from his North African prison camp and allowed to return to France, just as Rudy had predicted in his note to Jochen. Sylvain, who had been in a longtime relationship with a non-Jewish French woman, was allowed to return to the manufacturing firm for wooden toys that they operated in Agen, located in the southwest of France. Ostensibly, his skills and know-how were needed to keep the plant going, providing income for its workers. Many years later, in his video interview, my father recalled, "Upon leaving, as I learned from him, he had promised my brother that he would do all he could to win his liberation and have him brought back to France."

By early 1942, Rudy was also released from the camp; this was fortuitous because, as my father noted many years later, by the end of the war most of the camp inmates had "perished under the hot Sahara sun."

Upon his return to France, Sylvain arranged a position for Rudy. Since the Vichy police, in collaboration with the Gestapo, from time to time conducted raids to ferret out Jews in occupied France, Rudy carried false credentials identifying him as Robert Granier, a Frenchman.

What's more, Rudy had met Lydie Lalfert, a young woman whose family owned a summer residence in Agen. Rudy was smitten by the striking and vivacious twenty-two-year-old beauty, and, despite the risk of harboring a Jew with false papers, her parents almost immediately took steps protect their daughter's beau—who would become her husband after the war. As my father reported, Rudy was thus able to evade capture during the frequent police round-ups of Jews and their sympathizers. "On the farm was a dry well, some 30 meters deep, and he had a bed there, and food was supplied to him by my later sister-in-law with ropes. After the danger was over, he came up and surfaced."

MY GRANDFATHER SAMI, BROKEN AND EMACIATED, having survived hard labor in Buchenwald, was released on January 21, 1942, one week after he turned fifty-seven. The record on his "rap sheet" was stamped *Dikal*, a contraction of the words *Darf in kein anderes Lager*, meaning "not to be transferred to another camp." In the secret code of the Gestapo, this was a prescient euphemism for what was next in store for him.

After two months of incarceration, it was a bittersweet reunion with the distraught Helene. The Nazis essentially curtailed communication with the outside world, and she was cordoned off from all her loved ones. She fretted over Recha and Hanneli, who still had not been able to secure an exit visa to join Richard in England. And what of her sons? There was no news. And now, what future was there for her and Sami, whose frantic efforts to leave had been interrupted by his incarceration? Would he continue to search for an exit? The pending doom no doubt was palpable in her nightmares. Little did she realize the horror that would befall her and her husband less than four months later.

UNBEKNOWNST TO HELENE, ONE DAY PRIOR to Sami's release, on January 20, 1942, in an ornate villa in the Wannsee suburb of Berlin, a top-secret discussion occurred among the top echelon of the SS—the notorious military branch of the Nazi Party.

The meeting to implement what was termed "The Final Solution of the Jewish Question" was chaired by SS General Reinhard Heydrich, a top aide to SS leader Heinrich Himmler. Among the attendees was another notorious criminal—SS Lieutenant Colonel Adolf Eichmann, chief of Jewish Affairs for the state's security apparatus. The agenda for the so-called "Wannsee Conference" centered on the nuts and bolts of implementing the mass deportation and extermination of the Jewish people in the entire German Reich. With many of the state agencies and administrative bodies from occupied territories represented, the discussion covered the massive coordination required to move millions of human beings to concentration camps, mass killing factories, and subsequent disposal of corpses.

There is virtually no doubt that the subject of mass cremation had been raised in the context of the meeting, where attendees were told that J.A. Topf & Söhne, a former Erfurt-based manufacturer of municipal waste incinerators, was being engaged to produce the high-capacity crematoria needed to keep up with the demand. As it turned out, the initial estimate of cremating two hundred bodies daily proved insufficient; by September, as an internal corporate document unearthed after the war disclosed, even the five additional ovens with an eight- hundred daily capacity would not meet the demand at Auschwitz.[24]

ON MY FIRST VISIT TO ILMENAU with my parents in 1992, walking along the old town, we ran into an elderly man carrying a plastic sack of groceries. Seeing an unfamiliar face on what was likely his daily shopping route, he engaged my father in conversation. Learning that he was a native of Ilmenau, the son of the owners of the onetime Sandler store, the old man's face lit up in recognition.

"So you are the younger boy?" he asked in amazement. He proceeded to relate how he remembered last seeing my grandparents walking downhill from Goethestrasse, wearing the obligatory Star of David emblem on their overcoats. He did not inquire about their fate, nor did he relate how he had spent the war years. Nor did my father ask.

Indeed, if you lived in Ilmenau, it was impossible not to know the fate of the few remaining Jewish neighbors. It was evident to my grandparents as well—indeed in the brief message of a postal card addressed to Basel, in neutral Switzerland—that ended up in my father's trove of documents:

May 4, 1942

My dearest! We have received your message. We are glad that you are well. We are healthy, too. Your letters will unfortunately not reach us here, as we expect to leave Ilmenau next week. - Stay healthy and strong!

In heartfelt love and faithfulness

Yours Lenchen

Below was this brief rejoinder from my grandfather:

Sincerest and dearest regards, Your Sami

Expect to leave. A horrific understatement for the last postal card to be received from my grandparents, who in writing these words knew full well where they were headed in six days. They had gotten the order to report on the Jewish Sabbath, May 9, 1942, to the cattle auction hall in Weimar, where all the remaining Jews in Thuringia were being rounded up for the following morning's train transport—destination still unknown.

In all the research into the fate of Ilmenau's Jews conducted by my parents' friend Juliane Rauprich and others, there was no conclusive evidence of the final demise of my grandparents. All we know for sure is that meticulous records kept by the Nazi regime include a manifest for the Da27 transport that bears the names of Samuel Gronner and his wife, Helene Gronner née Sandler. We also know that the final destination of the train and its Jewish cargo—for that is how the Nazis treated them—was the ghetto in the eastern Polish town of Bełżyce. But no proof has been unearthed that Sami and Helene actually disembarked from the train.

On the basis of circumstantial evidence that emerged after German reunification, the fate Sami and Helene suffered in the end is unimaginable.

My main source for information on the Da27 is a website, *judenintemar.org*, launched by Dr. Sharon Meen, a Canadian academic and volunteer at the Vancouver Holocaust Education Center in Canada.

Through unearthed archival documents, correspondence, and witness testimony, the website has aggregated the chronology of events and experiences of the doomed passengers. Relying on the German National Archives, it reports:

> *On 30 April 1942, the authorities informed the Jewish Association of its role and duties in organizing the transport. On 4 May 1942, mayors received detailed instructions about the roundup of Jews in their individual municipalities; the mayors passed the orders on to the Jewish men and women: they were to pack one piece of luggage weighing 50 kg. and send it on ahead to Weimar by May 7th; their hair was to be cut; they were to buy train tickets for the journey in advance; and they were to be "in a clean condition" for the journey.*

The website quotes from a memoir describing their initial experience:

> *The assembly place for the deportees was Weimar's stock pen. Armed SA men guarded the entrance. Had the Nazis chosen this place to further humiliate us, to equate Jews with animals?*
>
> *The sour smell of fear mixed with cow dung and straw was overpowering. More and more people arrived carrying suitcases. Old and young, they lined up to have their papers examined. I had never been in a stock pen before. Along the wall were individual stalls designed to hold animals, and to the side stood a large scale. Beyond that were the railroad tracks.*[25]

The narrative continues in a dry, methodical manner that spares the reader the anguish, the stench of humanity stuffed into box cars like sardines in a can, the horror of looking into death's eyes with corpses of humans who had just died next to you.

> *Sometime between midnight and dawn on 10 May 1942, 513 men, women and children were loaded into cattle cars and transported to Leipzig where 287*

people joined the transport; then it was on to Chemnitz where 199 more people were herded onto the train. The exact destination was unknown until the last minute: in the initial plans, the destination of Train 'Da27', the train to carry the Thüringen Jews, was the all-purpose 'Trawniki,' a synonym for 'east,' near Lublin. It then became Izbica, a ghetto about 90 km southeast of Bełżyce. But just as the train left, the destination was finalized as Bełżyce. The transport travelled 1050 km to Lublin, arriving on May 12 1942.

The logistical planning required for such an ambitious undertaking reminds me of a lecture I heard years ago by Raul Hilberg, a noted Holocaust historian. He related how, in researching his book *The Destruction of European Jews,* he had spent an inordinate amount of time in the offices of the German railways, poring over memoranda and schedules from the wartime-era *Deutsche Reichsbahn*. The key thesis of his initially controversial work was that the Holocaust was the first instance of a highly industrial state harnessing its entire manufacturing and transport infrastructure for the sole purpose of mass murder.

It was as if Germany and all the countries it occupied were laid out as a giant toy train set, with materiel, supplies, and support personnel loaded and dispatched across the landscape in a highly coordinated fashion. Jews were collected into holding pens and then loaded like cargo onto freight cars destined to an archipelago of concentration camps and killing factories scattered throughout Germany and Poland.

IN A CODA TO THE ITINERARY of the hellish Da27 journey, there is this notation on Dr. Meen's website: "Because Bełżyce had no railway connection to Lublin, the men, women, and children had to walk at least 4-5 hours to reach Bełżyce, 24 km to the west of Lublin."

I only hope that Sami, recently released from hard labor at the Buchenwald concentration camp, and Helene, a long-suffering mother in deep anxiety over not knowing whether her sons were dead or alive, had not survived the arduous train ride. Through shrieks of other mothers and children, she fretted over her dear brother Willi, forced into a home for the aged in Frankfurt. What of her niece, Recha, and her precious Hanneli? Would they find a way out to be reunited with Richard in England?

What sins did we commit that you would ordain this fate upon us, merciful God, she likely prayed to drown out the moans and cries that grew incrementally louder with each stop, as more humanity was forced into the already tightly packed conveyance whose ultimate destination no one knew.

Even if they did survive the two-day train ride in the stench-filled rolling prison holding eighty or perhaps one hundred people, some already dead or dying beside them, I would be relieved if they had failed to reach the ghetto by collapsing from fatigue on this forced march that followed.

Or, possibly, in her anguish, Lenchen peered into the eyes of an armed Nazi guard, seeking a hint of any remaining humanity in his soul, beseeching him with her gaze to end her misery by shooting her and her husband right then and there. If that had been the case, I imagine that my grandparents would have by then welcomed such a gesture.

I NEVER CONFRONTED MY FATHER about how these nightmarish scenarios weighed on him after learning that his parents had perished.

But I do know that as soon as the war ended, he addressed an inquiry to the new Communist regime that the victorious Russians installed in Ilmenau—composed of self-described anti-Fascists, upstanding citizens of the GDR who considered themselves as fortunate to have been liberated from the Nazi yoke.

Let him explain in his own words how he reacted to the official news from the GDR authorities in his claim for compensation:

> *In our possession is an official communication of the people's police district office Ilmenau that concludes with the following laconic sentence: "It is to assume that the married couple Samuel and Helene Gronner had encountered death in the east because of their race."*

CHAPTER 10

Loss and Renewal

N ONE OF THE FOLDERS I SET ASIDE for miscellaneous items, I find a black-and-white snapshot, no larger than two by three inches, depicting a seated soldier in British battle dress khaki and sporting a field cap. He dwarfs the four petite young women astride him—two each to his left and right. His arms are outstretched behind the shoulders of the pair closest to him.

The spot is familiar to me from childhood. It is a bench on the Tel Aviv boardwalk along the Mediterranean, where the breakers peer through from behind the subjects' shoulders. To all appearances, it is just an ordinary bright day for relaxation at the seashore. The women are all dressed in white, including the white caps they are wearing—presumably they are nurses or some sort of medical professionals on their lunch break.

It is a serene photo as the five subjects smile for the benefit of the camera that freezes them in time.

The year is 1943.

AT THIS VERY MOMENT, FREIGHT CARS are crisscrossing the German Reich, bearing the human cargo destined for the high-capacity Topf & Söhne crematories in Auschwitz-Birkenau and other death factories.

By this time, my father's first cousin Recha, twenty-eight, and her beloved Hanneli, not yet five years old, have been swept up in Halle and taken to their deaths at Sobibor. Neither had a chance to be reunited with Richard Cohn, husband and father, whose efforts to get them to England had failed.

Wilhelm, founder of the Sandler family enterprise, forcefully confined to a home for the aged in Frankfurt after his brief residence with the Gronners in Ilmenau, has so far survived deportation to Terezin, where he had arrived on August 18, 1942. (He would live for another year until his deportation and death in Auschwitz in May 1944.)

Isidor Abraham, who in my research provided the clue to Willi's ingenious business model, is already dead—killed at age fifty-seven in Sachsenhausen; his wife and two children by then had also been killed in the Riga Ghetto in Latvia, having been deported from their home in Mühlhausen.

Samuel Gronner had fretted for his Austrian family at the outset of the *Anschluss*. His mother Auguste died in the spring of 1940 and was buried in the main cemetery, Zentralfriedhof. It turned out his worst fears about the Gronner clan had in fact materialized.

His own murder and that of his wife are as yet not known by the couple's sons; nor are Rudy and Jochen aware that the eighty-five-year-old widower Hermann Gronner, their paternal grandfather, was murdered in Terezin; or that three of their father's siblings—their uncle Wilhelm Gronner and aunts Antonie and Margit—died in the Maly Trostinec death camp near Minsk, Belarus; as did Margit's husband Edgar Friedenthal and their daughter Gertrude.

If ignorance is bliss, you can see it in the five smiling faces on the bench by the Tel Aviv seashore. I only recognize one among them: on the soldier's right sits my mother, at the time twenty-three-year-old Vera Bakel, a *Jecke* immigrant from Berlin. Because of her diminutive stature, her feet dangle child-like off the ground. The only clue about the man in the middle is my father's hand-written notation on a yellow Post-It note affixed to the back of the snapshot: *Our Shadchan Šani Steinmets with the girls at the T. Aviv Beach. 1943*

The Hebrew term *shadchan* means "matchmaker". The photo provides proof that this mutual acquaintance was the one who'd introduce Vera to Jochen, whom he likely met in the British army. Whatever happened thereafter to Šani is a mystery, because I do not recall ever meeting him among my parents' large circle of friends.

The simultaneous juxtaposition of romantic pursuits in Palestine and unspeakable events in Europe may appear unseemly, but it is a reality of time and place. Even as I write these lines, headlines about celebrity weddings and scandals abound alongside Instagram images of food creations, viral videos of cute children, funny dogs, and cats. But the cumulative effect of these vapid distractions is that they divert our attention from the horrific images of homeless vagrants in our cities, drowning refugees fleeing war, terrorism, famine, and emaciated toddlers in war-torn Yemen.

Thus it is perfectly normal for these young *Jecke* immigrants who had left Europe to live on in pursuit of romantic interests and new adventures with their similarly situated peers.

Vera had one advantage over Jochen, however. Her immediate family—comprised of parents, siblings, and even maternal grandparents—had all made it safely to Eretz Israel. Still living at home under imported *Jecke* norms, she had to abide by the strict rules set by her father; nonetheless, photos in the collection I have inherited provide ample evidence of her proclivity for fun with friends—including snap-shots of many unidentified young men haphazardly affixed long ago in the album from which photos were spilling like leaves at peak foliage time.

It was likely her lust for life and love of dance that attracted my dad to Vera, the eldest of the four children of Moritz and Leah Bakel, who had made the voyage from Berlin in 1938, and settled in Tel Aviv.

Under Jewish Agency and British immigration rules, Vera, having turned eighteen and no longer regarded as a dependent, was required to attend both *Hachshara,* a Zionist orientation for all newcomers, as well as a professional training course, so that she qualified for work immediately upon arrival in Palestine. As her parents and siblings left Berlin, she headed to Hamburg, where, under sponsorship of the Women's Inter-national Zionist Organization, she was trained as a practical pediatric nurse. Her family greeted her in Haifa when her ship eventually docked a few months later.

No doubt, this being wartime, the budding courtship was an on-and-off affair, active when Jochen was on furlough from the front, yet not interfering with Vera's social engagements with her circle of friends. (I remember my daughter once asking her grandmother about her mem-ories of the war years, and how I was startled when my mother linked those times to parties and attending dances organized for soldiers on leave in Tel Aviv.)

Vera was a big city girl, in contrast to Jochen's childhood experience in a small provincial town. Her tight-knit family was her source of com-fort and safety from which she never strayed, even in old age.

The Biblical command to honor one's father and mother—in this case, the paternal fidelity—was well ingrained in Vera's personality as well as those of her sisters Mady and Esther.

Their brother Paul was not as compliant, and was first to morph into a committed pioneer *kibbutznik* while his sisters remained close to the nest in Tel Aviv. As part of his *Hachshara* experience, he was sent to Ramat Yochanan, an established kibbutz on the outskirts of Haifa. As was typical, his group was brought together with other recent European arrivals who were undergoing similar orientation in other settlements, and at one of those occasions he met a Viennese-born teenager named Dvora Plawes, who was then part of a parallel program south of Tel Aviv. Upon turning eighteen, and having no close relatives in Palestine, she joined the Ramat Yochanan community, where she had a personal acquaintance in Paul. Dvora and Paul became a couple and tried another communal settlement, but returned to Ramat Yochanan and eventually married.

To his father's chagrin, Paul's decision to assume the Hebrew name Shimshon Elath meant that the Bakel family name would be retired; Moritz expected all his three daughters to eventually marry and take on their husbands' surname. I surmise that Shimshon's Zionist zeal motivated Moritz to Hebraisize his given birth name, "Moische," as he was called by his Yiddish-speaking kin in Kalisz, Poland—prior to his move to Berlin, where he had assumed a cosmopolitan Berlin persona as Moritz Bakel.

Bakel family get-togethers in Tel Aviv were frequent, centered on meals created, not by Vera's mother Leah, but rather by her grandmother Rivka Steinlauf. It fell to Rivka to be the homemaker, as Leah had borne four children in rapid succession between age eighteen through twenty-five. The assignation of Rivka as the family cook continued in Eretz Israel. I suspect that was one reason my mother's cooking skills rarely rose above average, though she did excel in baking plum pies.

In recalling one of her first dates with my future dad, my mother often told the story of asking Jochen to meet her in front of her parents' building on Ness Ziona Street. When she returned after work and didn't find him, she stormed into the upstairs apartment and was shocked to find her date sitting with her mother in the parlor.

My father's attraction to Vera, I believe, was not only to her outgoing and upbeat personality but to what people would refer to as the baggage couples bring into a relationship—something he now craved, namely the intimate family relationships he had left behind in Europe.

In some way, he took to the Bakels in the manner Sami had to the Sandler clan upon venturing away from his roots in Silesia and arriving in a new land filled with opportunities.

To Moshe's discerning eyes, the lanky, German-born British soldier towering by more than a foot over Vera made for an odd-looking couple, but Jochen proved worthy of marrying his eldest daughter. For her, the blessing from her father sealed the deal.

The wedding plans depended on the cooperation of Jochen's commanding officer. By 1944, British allied forces had essentially defeated Germany's Afrika Korps. Britain now controlled North Africa as General Montgomery led the Eighth Army across the Mediterranean to join the Allied invasion of Italy. Perhaps it was an opportune time for his commanding officer to grant leave to one of his Palestine-based Royal Engineers in order to get hitched, and the date was set for Tuesday, October 10, 1944.

To all outward appearances, this was a normal Jewish wedding, the bride dressed in white, and the groom in full military dress. It still being wartime, however, overseas travel from Germany and France would have made it impossible for any Gronners to participate. No evidence exists that my father had tried to reach his parents, his brother, nor any family that had stayed behind. He likely knew it was for naught.

That's why, as the two families were formally joined, none of Jochen's paternal blood relatives were in attendance. In the group photo of the wedding party, only his maternal side is represented with uncles, cousins and their spouses.

It is a celebratory image of survivors—portraying those, who, through foresight, good fortune and tenacity—were saved by having made the journey to Eretz Israel.

From the Sandler side, sitting in the first row, are Meta Sandler, widow of my father's uncle Isidor, who was fatally injured in the Kaiser's army during the First World War; next to her sits her brother-in-law Bernhard, Jochen's uncle who owned the Sandler affiliated store in Sonneberg with his late wife Paula; Bernhard's son—my father's first cousin Sigfried—is captured in the wedding photo, but curiously, his older brother Heinz is not. Standing behind the bride and groom is Tante Meta (Miriam), wife of the attorney Dr. Georg Sandler, also in the wedding party along with their children Rachel, Meir, and Daniel; and Judith Sandler, a daughter of Isidor, is there, as is her sister Klaire, along with her husband Herbert Wertheimer.

I see two children but can only identify Margalit, the five-year-old daughter of Siegfried and Hanna Grünspan, who tragically died the following year from an allergic reaction to an insect bite. Yet I clearly recognize Vera's siblings—Shimshon and his partner Dvora; Esther, the youngest, and Mady with her husband "Kuba", a nickname for Jacob. Leah Bakel is to the bride's right, while Moshe and Kalman Steinlauf, her grandfather, sit to the groom's left. Kalman's wife and family cook had previously died.

After a brief honeymoon at the seaside resort (and favorite *Jecke* enclave) Nahariya, Jochen and Vera rented a small apartment near the Bakel home. During the ongoing prosecution of the war against the Axis powers, Jochen continued in active military service in the North African theater.

Meanwhile, militant Zionist organizations opposed to the immigration ban had hatched an insurgency campaign in February 1944 to end the Mandatory regime. Led by the Irgun, known by the initials IZL, a contraction of the Hebrew name for National Military Organization, the Zionist movement intensified insurgent actions against the British military, targeting police stations, prisons, and military barracks—at times in coordination with the Haganah.

In response, just prior to Germany's surrender on my father's twenty-fifth birthday, Britain dispatched its Sixth Airborne Division to fight the insurgents, but this only intensified the armed rebellion.

My father was discharged from the British Army in 1946 and, like most Jewish soldiers who fought with Britain against Germany, was almost immediately put to work in support of the insurgency in a clandestine munitions factory in Tel Aviv.

On July 22, 1946, Jerusalem's King David Hotel, housing the Military High Command, was heavily damaged in a massive explosion set off by a small team of operatives from the Irgun. In order to minimize civilian losses, a member of the strike team phoned in the following message: "I am speaking on behalf of the Hebrew underground. We have placed an explosive device in the hotel. Evacuate it at once—you have been warned." The French Consulate next to the hotel was also warned in advance. When the dust settled, the incident had claimed ninety-one fatalities, including twenty Britons, forty-one Arabs, seventeen Jews and five foreigners.[26]

As the insurgency continued through the following year, my father, now a civilian, found a job as director of manufacturing at *Haboreg*, a nut-and-bolt factory outside Tel Aviv. He commuted to work on a British-made motorcycle, which he claimed to have "found" while in the military.

On Rosh Hashanah of the following year, September 15, 1947, Vera gave birth to a son who was given the Hebrew biblical name of Amnon. My middle name, Shmuel, was bestowed upon me in memory of my grandfather Sami, who by then was known to have been killed somewhere "in the east," along with his wife.

As I had heard many times from my Opa Moshe, my birth on the first day of the Jewish New Year was a most glorious event of seemingly heavenly proportions: He was in synagogue upon receiving word of the arrival of his first male grandchild. Undoubtedly, he had celebrated the previous year's birth of my cousins Avital, born to Dvora and Shimshon, and Daphne, born six months earlier to Mady and Kuba; but in his mind, the arrival of the first male descendant of the first generation born in Eretz Israel merited full attention from the entire congregation crowded in the house of worship, and he danced for joy among the pews to spread his good fortune.

Throughout the years, as a consequence of my having been born on the first day of the Jewish New Year 5708, my family celebrated my birthday on Rosh Hashanah, rather on September 15.

THE BEGINNING OF MY INFANCY was marked by great stress on my parents in light of continuing inter-Palestinian strife and economic challenges. It was a time of food rations and intensified Jewish-Arab hostilities sparked by the November 29 United Nations adoption of a resolution to partition the British Mandate territory into three sectors—one Jewish, one Arab, and a third internationally protected zone encompassing Jerusalem and Bethlehem.

The hostilities between the Jewish and Arab communities in Palestine led to a renewed phase of civil war that my father had encountered upon his arrival in 1936—a simmering conflict between Arabs and Jews that was subdued through the end of the Second World War but was then reignited.

Emboldened by the United Nations resolution, Israel declared its independence on May 14, 1948, as the democratic national home of the Jewish people within the frontiers the UN had outlined. The following day, the civil war erupted into a full-fledged international conflict as the nascent state mounted a vigorous defense against the invading armies of its immediate neighbors—Egypt, Jordan, and Syria—with support from Iraqi forces.

For my father, the ensuing war of independence blurred the distinction between civilian and military activities, as the entire nation was enlisted in its existential fight.

My father related his personal role in helping secure Israel's victory:

> I was called into the Hagana headquarters and told that the Israeli army needed specialists in the drawing and heat treatment of heavy gun barrels. Since I passed two related courses while in the British Army, I was one of the very few Palestinians who knew anything about artillery. They had none, and barely had guns. I was "requested" to help create the artillery of the Israeli army.
>
> A colleague of mine named Danziger had gone through the same courses, and we were both working in the nut-and-bolt factory. There were no skilled laborers after the outbreak of the War of Independence. The boss went to the High Command and pleaded with them that, if he lost both of us, he might as well shut down the plant. Our plant was vital in manufacturing of drawing shells for the Davidka, an Israeli-produced mortar. So we split our military service—six months for each man.

CHAPTER 11

My Sabra Childhood

I N A NOW-TATTERED PHOTO ALBUM of my childhood, my mother
meticulously noted, in German, that I was first able to sit alone at
eight months, and to stand unassisted at eleven. From a birth weight
of 2.9 kilograms, I became a four-month-old weighing more than six
kilos by December 24, 1947. Apparently she lost interest in filling in the
pre-printed form after three months, as there is no further entry of such
details.

Nonetheless, using photo corners, she did secure visual evidence of
my growth onto the black pages of the album: at three and a half-months
in my crib; being held on Oma's lap, with my grandfather, in a dapper
suit and dark fedora sitting beside her. She had used a light-colored pencil on the black paper to write a caption for another photo in German:
Amnon and his great-grandfather, as the happy infant sits on the lap of Kalman
Steinlauf, who likewise sports a jacket and tie, in true *Jecke* fashion.

Who would imagine that some of the latter infant photos of me at
eight and nine months were taken while Israel was battling for its very

existence? The impression left by the snapshots is that Tel Aviv was a serene city where a new mother could safely bring her son to visit with the grandparents down the street, or stroll to a park to pose for a photo of an elder holding a third- and even fourth-generation descendant.

The photo album provides a timeline for when my parents left Tel Aviv, since I see a photo of me when I was eleven months old.

The location takes me back to my earliest memories of childhood in a new housing development that was rapidly constructed in the Tel Aviv suburb of Holon, the name of which is rooted in the Hebrew word for "sand," indicative of the sandy dunes that stretched from our new home south to Rishon L'Zion and west to the seashore at Bat Yam.

My parents called our neighborhood *Shikun Chadash*—new apartment complex—whose residents consisted primarily of young *Jeckes* who were just starting the post-war Baby Boomer generation of Israelis. The housing was utilitarian more than picturesque, consisting of single story dwellings with many adjoining units sharing a bathroom. The living arrangement promoted strong bonds among neighbors, for whom German was the *lingua franca*. Lifelong bonds were formed in those days, and the seeds of friendship sown in Holon blossomed into bonds that crossed oceans and were even passed on to my generation.

We were too young to understand the wartime footing under which the nascent state existed, helped by the fact that *Shikun Chadash* was a cocoon sheltered from the danger of the ongoing war. (That was not true of our family in Jerusalem.) In fact, we were not yet aware, in 1948, that Holon had been the site of a battle between the local Haganah forces and Arabs in the neighboring village of Tel Arish, just south of Jaffa.

As young children, we felt no perceptible change once the armistice was signed in 1949, creating the international frontiers that held until the Six-Day War in 1967.

We lived in a magical land in which we had friends just like us and everyone got along famously. More than seventy years later, my friend Roni Benjamin and I reminisce about the snowfall of January 1950, when our neighborhood was transformed into a winter wonderland. I still remember how I was completely awed by the rare meteorological event in Israel's coastal plain. My father often recalled my first experience with the fallen snow when I ran into the house excitedly yelling, "Aba, come quick and see the white sand that fell from the sky!"

THE END OF MILITARY HOSTILITIES allowed my father to refocus his attention on professional career advancement. His star at Haboreg was rising, and his experience in the British Army and Haganah had led his management to recommend him for a mission to the United States under sponsorship the Histadrut labor organization, in coordination with its American counterpart, the AFL-CIO. The delegation's objective was to learn about the latest metalworking techniques used in the United States in order to apply them to modernize Israel's manufacturing sector.

Joining this mission as a representative, not only of his employer, but also of Israel's leading labor organization, caused my father to shed his Jochen persona and assume a newly fashionable Israeli identity. Among the family and his personal friends, he would remain Jochen, but to professional colleagues he would henceforth become the Hebrew-literate Yochanan Gronner.

My father boarded a ship bound for New York in March 1950. During his absence, my mother became my main interlocutor, and that is how, in true *Jecke* tradition, German became my first language.

This immersion in German as a toddler during my father's three-month absence culminated in a moment that I would have to live down for the rest of his life. Upon his return from America with all his professional Hebrew-speaking peers, the former *Jecke* was met by his *Sabra* (native-born Israeli) son who belted out in the shrillest German voice, "*Aba, wo warst Du denn so lange?*" The question of where his dad had been for so long was natural for a child to ask, but the fact that it was uttered in flawless German within earshot of his Israeli colleagues haunted me for years as my father retold the anecdote time and again.

Aba had diligently applied himself during his study tour of the machine shop at a General Motors plant in Detroit. Upon his return he wrote a technical paper entitled, "Screw Manufacturing in America" that became a chapter in a compilation of reports by other mission delegates to the United States, Switzerland, and Britain. I found a tattered copy of the *Histadrut*-published paperback in the materials I inherited, including a group photo on page 417 where he is pictured.

Still, it was not strictly a professional development visit. Having made the journey, my father was determined to connect with family members who had settled in America.

Upon arrival in New York, he took time to see my mother's sister Mady, who had emigrated from Israel the prior year with her husband Kuba and their daughter Daphne.

He told me years later that he had failed in his attempt to see the sons of Uncle Emil Gronner, who had left Silesia seven years after Sami, landing in America in 1914.

Also settling in the Bronx was Jochen's Aunt Rosa, his father's surviving sister, and her husband Leo Selinger. The couple was able to leave Vienna with their son Fritz, who subsequently Americanized his name to Fred while serving in the U.S. Army during the war.

Aba did not manage to make it to Los Angeles, where another of Sami's siblings, Uncle Salo, had settled with his wife Erna, having reached

America in nineteen 1939 by way of Shanghai and Manila. However, since he was in Detroit, my father made a point of getting to Chicago and reuniting with Wilhelm Sandler's daughter—his cousin Ruth—and her husband Fred Weil, as well as their sons Stephen, born in Germany, and the American-born Peter.

Reconnecting with his relatives in the United States, and seeing how they were thriving, likely got my father thinking about one day following suit and pursuing the American dream. But that was then. In the short term, he had to return to his wife and son in Israel. For now, he would help turn the Jewish homeland into an economic success story, contributing in his own way by applying the advanced metalworking skills he had acquired.

FOR ALL I KNEW, LIFE IN HOLON continued to be blissful. My parents socialized with their Jecke circle of friends while I befriended their children who became my playmates. I recall riding our tricycles like a tiny tot version of the Hell's Angels. My buddies Roni, Dani, and Moshe, and I were inseparable, and I recall enjoying beach days in Bat Yam with our mothers. Our cluster also included some girls whom I tolerated, especially at various birthday parties.

My father worked long hours, commuting by motorcycle to work each day, and as it grew dark, I listened for the rumbling of the BSA signaling his return. By the time I was four, I was allowed to sit on the gas tank in front of my dad, as my mother sat in the rear seat on excursions to Oma and Opa in Tel Aviv.

All that changed when my sister was born on March 23, 1952. My parents named the baby Tamar Helena, in memory of our grandmother.

The motorcycle could no longer transport all four of us—and significantly, our living quarters would soon not be big enough to support another person.

About that time, we moved to a brand-new development constructed by the government-supported Rural and Suburban Settlement Company, referred to by everyone as Rassco. We moved into the first phase of the project, Rassco Alef.

Our new home was an upstairs apartment in a two-story white-washed building occupied below by the Avivi family. We reached our flat by climbing an outdoor staircase. The building housed four units on two levels, one side a mirror image of the other.

To the rear of our small back yard were other apartment units in a different style—two stories high but elongated blocks with adjoining apartment doors—perhaps a half dozen, not unlike motels I had come to know in America.

Our house was set back from a new Histadrut Street that had recently been paved over the sand. Across the road there were nothing but sand dunes—an ideal place to sit around bonfires that are traditional during the *Lag B'Omer* holiday.

The street was so new that I remember the day a crew came to install a bus stop, enabling the new residents to use public transit. But we did not need such conveyance. Unlike most of our neighbors, we were mobile thanks to the sidecar my father had purchased to allow my mother and sister to ride while I sat behind him on the BSA. My father stored the motorcycle and sidecar under a carport in the front yard.

What memories I retain of our years in Rassco Alef are idyllic. The bulk of my interaction with other children came through our back yard, which led past the homes behind us into Wolfson Street. This neighborhood was my entire world, and the friendships I developed were primarily with children of my parents' *Jecke* crowd.

The most lasting of those relationships is the second-generation bond I still maintain with the daughter of my mother's closest *Jecke* friend Irene.

Like my mother, Irene had become a pediatric practical nurse when the pair met in 1942 while both were pushing prams in Tel Aviv's London Square. Irene, who hailed from Königsberg, had no immediate family in Palestine, and her bond with Vera led the Bakels to regard her as part of their family. (There she is in the family photo of my grandparents' silver anniversary.) In return, Irene referred to Moshe and Leah as "Papa" and "Mama."

Irene had married Erich Mamson, a *Jecke* from Wuppertal, who had come to Palestine by way of Italy, where he had been sent to await a reunion with his older brother. Because of his diminutive stature, his Italian comrades had resorted to calling him Pico, a name that stuck for the rest of his life.

Reni (as we all called her) and Pico had a daughter Gabriella nine months after I was born. Later, when her brother Eran was born, Reni had always referred to me as *Mein Zweiter Sohn* (my second son), and as far back as I can remember, I regarded Gabi as my other sibling—such was the bond between our families.

My parents' circle of *Jecke* friends encompassed both those from the old neighborhood and Rassco residents, and as a consequence I befriended their children. Across the street and perpendicular to the Mamsons' block-style building stood a similar motel-style apartment house along Wolfson Street where the widow Herta Reich lived. Her son Roni became one of my playmates. The Schweitzer family, whose children were also named Tamar and Amnon, lived there. Roni Löwenstein, whose father was a policeman, became another in our group of friends. Avi Avivi was my downstairs friend, and occasionally my parents socialized with *Shikun Chadash* couples like the Grünbaums, whose older son

Dani remained a friend, as well as the Lembergs and Grünspans, whose daughters, respectively Irit and Edna, were my contemporaries.

OUR IDYLLIC EXISTENCE WAS SUDDENLY DISRUPTED in the fall of 1956 when the Israel Defense Forces activated its reserves—including my father—for the Sinai campaign. My most lasting memory of those days is the recruitment of us children in helping fortify our school building by filling bags of sand and piling them up to seal the open spaces above the walls along the exterior walkways connecting the classrooms. We were also taught to practice nighttime blackouts by ensuring that curtains were drawn in order to disorient potential enemy aircraft. Fortunately, no Egyptian plane reached Israel during the brief hostilities that saw Gen. Moshe Dayan lead the IDF to occupy the entire Sinai Peninsula in a matter of days.

In December of that year, my father returned home from the front. As he later recalled:

> It was around the time of Chanukah and I was anxious to return home to my children and wife. I had no money, and I asked my commander how I would get home from the Sinai. He offered me an Israeli pound. I somehow made it home. After being away for four months, I see my kids sitting on the stairs to my house. I was in rags. They hugged me and both asked, "Aba, what did you get us for Chanukah?"

I don't believe this to be true. For many years, he had told the tale, always claiming that it was I whom he disappointed by coming home empty-handed. Viewing his video testimony for the first time, I heard him embellish the tale by including my four-year-old sister in the narrative.

In my assessment, this was a complete fib because, to this very day, the idea of Chanukah gifts feels alien to me—a practice that began in the diaspora in response to the commercialization of Christmas. During my childhood, I never expected more than getting treats of gold-foiled chocolate coins known as *Chanukah Geld* and joining my schoolmates at Chanukah parties highlighted by a generous supply of jelly donuts—known as *sufganyot*.

That I would have expected more in those days is inconceivable. Living in Holon, never understanding or ever seeing Christmas festivities in the Christian enclaves of Nazareth, Jerusalem, and Bethlehem, I had not even heard of Santa Claus, let alone how children waited for his nocturnal visits to deliver presents to eight-year-olds like me.

I think my father concocted this fiction as his rationale for a decision that would alter the fate of our family. His following videotaped remarks are far closer to the truth:

> *I have been in this country for twenty years. What do I have to show for myself? When I got upstairs, my wife presented me with some twenty bills from the grocery store. I asked, "Didn't you get paid from the national social security in my absence? You are supposed to receive my soldier's pay."*
>
> *I owned a motorcycle—a luxury in Israel. I drove to the Bank Hapoalim in town where I knew everyone. "I need a loan for six hundred pounds," I said. With that I was able to pay off my debt, and I made up my mind at that moment. I no longer want to be here. I am ready to leave Israel.*

Hermann Gronner, father of Samuel Gronner

Meyer Sandler, father of Wilhelm Sandler and Helene Gronner, among others

Close-up, Helene Gronner and son Rudy Gronner from travel document below, 1916

Travel document, 1916

Vienna-based Gronner family in photo montage that includes the German branch, including Samuel, Jochen, and Rudy at far left and Helene Gronner, top center.

Rudy Gronner, sixth from left, in Ilmenau´s primary school

The Gronner-Sandler-Grünspan clan at a typical summer gathering at the Baltic seashore. Front row, from left: Helene, Samuel, Jochen, and Rudy Gronner; Wilhelm and Ruth Sandler, center.

Samuel Gronner

Jochen and Rudy Gronner shown at the site of the new
Wilhelm Sandler store prior to its completion in 1929

Family members gather in 1935 for the engagement of Ruth Sandler
and Fritz Weil, front row, right. Standing, Helene Gronner, second from left,
Samuel Gronner, fifth, and Jochen Gronner, center.

Jochen Gronner as a teenager.

Photo commemorating the March, 1938, visit
Rudi and Sami made to Jochen in "Eretz Israel."

Rudy and his parents

In happier times, a Sandler family gathering. From left: Paula Grünspan, Wilhelm Sandler, Georg Sandler. Recha Grünspan, Helene and Samuel Gronner, and Ruth Sandler. Paula died in 1935; Georg and Ruth survived the Holocaust by emigrating.

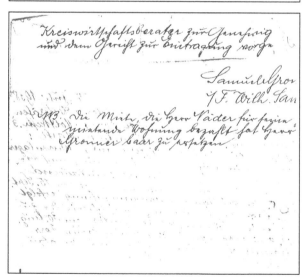

Samuel Gronner's handwritten proposal to transfer title of his Wilhelm Sandler business to Hillmar Näder, a certified member of the NSDAP, in accordance with the 1938 Nuremberg Law stripping Jews from the right to property. Attached is a Sept. 25, 1947, certification by the Ilmenau municipality, that Näder had reported that Samuel Gronner was subject to registration until December 15, 1939, when he and his wife were forced to relocate to a so-called "Jew House" at 11 Goethestrasse.

Exterior of the former Wilhelm Sandler store during its
ownership by Nazi Party member Hillmar Näder

The same building as it appears today

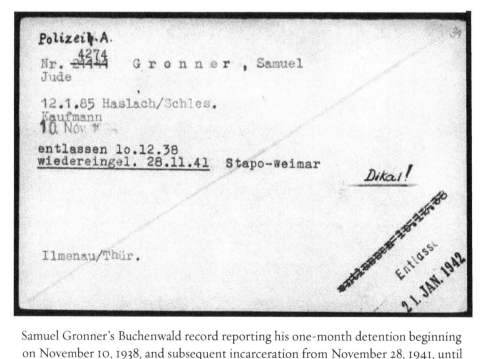

Postcard from Helene and Samuel Gronner dated May 4, 1942, It states,
Your letters will unfortunately not reach us here, as we expect to leave Ilmenau next week.
Five days later, they boarded a train to their certain death.

Polizei-A.

Nr. ~~4444~~ 4274   G r o n n e r , Samuel
Jude

12.1.85 Haslach/Schles.
Kaufmann
10. Nov ~~1~~

entlassen lo.12.38
wiedereingel. 28.11.41   Stapo-Weimar

Dikal!

Ilmenau/Thür.

Entlass. 21. JAN. 1942

Samuel Gronner's Buchenwald record reporting his one-month detention beginning
on November 10, 1938, and subsequent incarceration from November 28, 1941, until
January 21, 1942. The handwritten notation indicates he is not to be held
in another concentration camp.

Jochen´s British-issued identity card.

Jochen, sitting in front, with British Army Royal Engineers

Jochen on subsequent duty in North Africa

Rudy, left, on duty in 1940 with the French Legion in Saida, Morocco

Šani Steinmetz, who introduced Vera Bakel, on his right in the photo, to Joachim Gronner

The young couple

Yochanan Gronner explains the workings of a modified weapon used by the Haganah.

Wedding of Vera Bakel and Jochen Gronner

The fearsome foursome in Holon. Front to rear, Roni Benjamin, Moshe Chevroni, Dani Grünbaum (Ganor), Amnon Gronner

The brothers Rudy and John Gronner, in Bergenfield, New Jersey

SANDLER/GRÜNSPAN BRANCH
(Only main characters included)
(*) Denotes killed during Holocaust

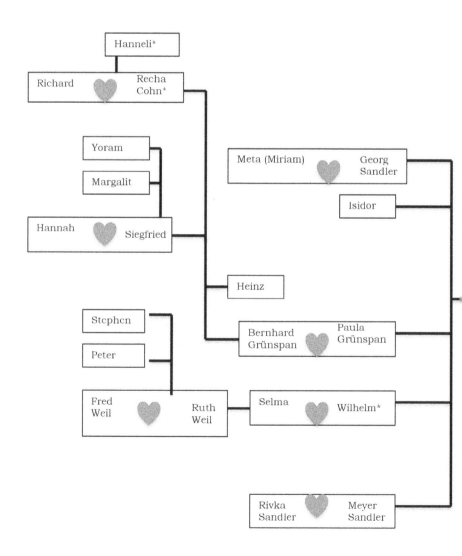

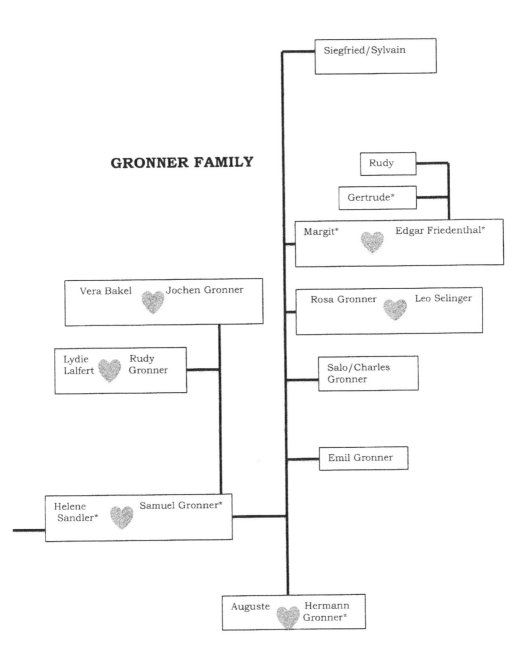

GRONNER FAMILY

Siegfried/Sylvain

Rudy

Gertrude*

Margit* Edgar Friedenthal*

Vera Bakel Jochen Gronner

Rosa Gronner Leo Selinger

Lydie Lalfert Rudy Gronner

Salo/Charles Gronner

Emil Gronner

Helene Sandler* Samuel Gronner*

Auguste Hermann Gronner*

CHAPTER 12

Yerida

The Hebrew word *Aliyah* means "an upward movement." In Jewish ritual, the term is applied when one is called to recite a particular weekly selection in the cycle of Torah readings. It is deemed an honor to be called up to publicly recite the words inscribed on the parchment that makes up the Torah scroll.

In a similar vein, when diaspora Jews decide to settle in the land of Israel, they are making *Aliyah*—going up to the Holy Land. Israelis call the newcomers *olim*—Jews who rise upward by returning to the ancestral land two millennia after the ancient Romans dispersed the Israelites throughout their empire.

The opposite of *Aliyah* is called *Yerida,* a "downward movement." In the 1950's, the idea of leaving the newly re-established national homeland of the Jewish people was severely frowned upon by the Zionist establishment. In their eyes, the task of building a Jewish state had just begun, and much work remained—building housing, expanding agriculture, and creating an industrial base. Anyone leaving was deemed selfish for placing self-interest above the nation's needs. These individuals were referred to as "yordim", and the term had come to take on negative connotations.

Yerida was not a topic openly discussed among Israelis, but among the Bakel relatives and some of my parents' tightly-knit *Jecke* crowd it apparently was an open secret, whispered about discreetly only among those who seriously mulled the idea of abandoning Herzl's Zionist dream of a national home for the world's persecuted Jews. Like my father, some came to believe that they had sacrificed their youth to creating the state. Now that they had growing families of their own, they sensed an imperative to reap the benefits afforded by the post-war Western economies for the next generation—most notably in the United States.

As far as I understood at the time, Yochanan Gronner was outwardly a typical union man whose socialist outlook had been shaped by *Hashomer Hatza'ir* and the influences of mentors and peers he had encountered in the Haganah. I recall the time of the national elections in 1955, a period that saw dissent against *Mapai,* the dominant Labour Party. My father was active in a leftist political movement called *Achdut Ha'avoda*, the United Workers Party, which sought to elect a Knesset delegation of pro-union advocates different from the *Mapai,* led by then-Prime Minister Moshe Sharett, who had succeeded the first Knesset leader, David Ben-Gurion.

I remember the day my dad took me along when he was part of a team in charge of setting up an *Achdut Ha'Avodah* political rally in downtown Jaffa.

As an eight-year-old, I didn't understand much of what was going on. But I took in the spectacle after climbing the stairs with him to the second floor of a nondescript building. I peered out over the ledge of a huge window overlooking an open expanse adjacent to a busy street. The glass and frame had been completely removed and I was able to look out as hundreds of people gathered below. My father's assignment was to set up the microphone and public address system.

The rally went on for a while, with speakers exhorting the crowd and eliciting vocal responses. But at one point, a speaker said something that upset some people in the crowd below, and suddenly we were being pelted with tomatoes through the open window. This was my first exposure to Israeli politics in action. It also formed my first impression of the *Herut* party, whose supporters were behind the tomato bombs.

It is said that when three Jews congregate, you can have as many as five opinions. Such is the nature of Israeli politics, where parties come and go and coalesce into rival blocs on the right and left.

In the national election for the Third Knesset, no less than nine parties vied for the 120 legislative seats, splitting a grand total of 853,259 eligible votes. My father's party won ten seats, compared to forty for *Mapai* and fifteen for *Herut.*[27]

Though my father was intimately involved in building Israeli democracy, he was now beginning the plot to leave it all behind by taking his family abroad.

UPON BEING DISCHARGED FROM his army service in February 1957, Aba asked Rudy to contact the West German consulate in Paris on his behalf and apply for a claim of restitution. In order to avoid any possible scrutiny, my father asked that no official mail from Germany be sent to Holon, lest anyone got wind of his plan to emigrate. He preferred that Rudy become the conduit and that all relevant correspondence to Israel bear Rudy's return address in Paris.

The secrecy of the scheme to leave was not limited to keeping nosy neighbors and my father's colleagues at *Haboreg* in the dark. To avoid being stained with the *yordim* epithet, our parents sought to protect us with a myth; telling my sister and me that we were going on a brief visit to France, where we would meet our Onkel Rudy and Tante Lydie and our French cousin Jean-Luc.

The preparations took several months, until the letter from Rudy arrived. "He notified me in August 1957 that everything was in order, and asked what I wanted to do," my father recalled. "I told him we will come there. When I received my exit visa, we left." The date of departure from Haifa aboard the *Theodor Herzl* was September 10, 1957. I was scheduled to start fourth grade, but it did not dawn on me to ask why I would be missing the beginning of the school year. I guess I imagined that a voyage to France on a big ocean liner would be a great experience and would make great fodder for the travelogue I would recount to my schoolmates upon my return. As it turned out, that day would never come.

I WAS TOO YOUNG TO REALIZE IT at the time, but in retrospect I was witness to my father's metamorphosis from an ardent pioneer dedicated to building a model socialist Jewish national homeland into an aspiring entrepreneur who would strive to reap the benefits of capitalism that he had tasted during his visit to America.

The first evidence of this transformation came during a layover in Naples. As we were about to disembark, he told me to put on his sport jacket and to wear it off the ship like an oversized coat. In all the jacket pockets he had stuffed packs of cigarettes that he had purchased onboard in the duty-free shop. My sister remained behind, being cared for in the ship's nursery school while I accompanied my parents.

The three of us had been wandering on foot through various alleyways when my father engaged a woman in conversation. There appeared to be some haggling going on; then she stepped away and disappeared into a doorway, presumably leading to her flat, because she returned shortly thereafter with a wad of Italian currency that she handed to my father. That led him to extract packs of cigarettes from the jacket he was wearing, a stash of others from my mother's purse, as well as the load that was hidden inside the pockets of the jacket I was wearing.

The transaction completed, and with a load of Italian *lire* in his wallet, he led us to Naples' shopping area to make his first major purchase with the currency conversion and profits earned from marking up the price he had paid for the duty-free cigarettes. His winnings consisted of Italian shoes for his entire family—something he could scarcely have afforded on his earnings at *Haboreg*, even in his supervisory role.

His gait revealed the palpable joy he had just felt on his venture into the illicit black market for tobacco products, and the new shoes in the bundles he happily carried were proof of the immediate payback for his entrepreneurial risk-taking.

Upon returning to the *Theodor Herzl*, he discovered one flaw in his scheme: the shoes he had purchased for my sister did not fit. To my mother's chagrin, he decided to go back to the store and exchange Tami's shoes. Ima begged him to forget about it, fearing he would never find the store again and miss the scheduled departure. Undeterred, he returned to the store and reappeared with the replacement shoes, whistling with self-confidence. He strolled up the gangplank just as the ship's horn sounded our departure for Marseilles.

AS I NOW REFLECT ON OUR DISEMBARKATION in the French Mediterranean port city, I can only conclude from the intervening years that the experience triggered an involuntary period of amnesia in me. Beyond fleeting visions and momentary experiences still etched into my mind, I suspect that, from that moment on, I began repressing places, events, and even the people I met. Little remains in my vault of memories of my family's two-year sojourn in Europe.

Yes, I recall being struck by Onkel Rudy's uncanny resemblance to Aba, even mannerisms so familiar to me, like the way both shook their bellies when laughing. My six-year-old cousin with the exotic name of Jean-Luc was reclusive and shy, not eager to communicate, not that either of us could converse—I couldn't speak French, nor could he in German or Hebrew. Did he interact with Tami? I have no recollection. My aunt Lydie greeted us warmly—my first exposure to the French practice of planting a kiss on both cheeks.

I have a vague memory of traveling to Paris by train. My next recollection is riding in the back of Onkel Rudy's Peugeot along a wide Paris boulevard and coming to a sudden, screeching halt to avoid a collision with the car ahead—a boy, a recent arrival from North Africa (Morocco or Tunisia?)—had darted into the street and been run over by a taxicab ahead of us. I do not recall seeing the injured child.

I think we briefly stayed in a hotel—"l'Opéra" sticks in my mind as either the place of lodging or the neighborhood. But it may have been the place we domiciled on a later visit to Paris.

It is all a blank to me now. At some point, we packed up our belongings again and boarded a train for Frankfurt. The next phase of my father's plan to seek reparations for the murder of his parents was to return to Germany, which at the time meant West Germany, since his hometown of Ilmenau was in the hands of the Soviet-controlled German Democratic Republic.

MY RECOLLECTION OF FRANKFURT in the fall of 1957 is projected in my mind as a black and white film, devoid of color, dreary, a landscape of rubble that had lain fallow since the Allied bombings ceased more than a decade earlier. My first introduction to the city was a ground floor apartment in a rooming house that Germans refer to as a *Pension*. The building, perhaps three stories high, abutted an open lot scattered with broken bricks and stones, likely the remains of what had been an adjacent residence for several families.

The stark contrast to my home in Holon was jarring as I perused the drab scene, longing for the whitewashed buildings reflecting the bright Middle Eastern sun, and the voices of giddy children reverberating throughout the neighborhood. I suppose I was homesick, but I can't remember whether I brought this up with my parents.

My sister and I had most assuredly been advised that my mother's friend Irene Mamson and her family had already reached Frankfurt ahead of us, and that she had in fact arranged for us to initially stay at the rooming house. I have no recollection of this sequence of events, but I do remember that our families of *yordim* regularly congregated in Frankfurt. It was as if a swarm of *Jecke* bees had left their hive in Israel and reconvened in Germany on their way to their ultimate goal—reaching America.

My photo collection includes mementos of the encounters my parents had with their circle of *Jeckes* and their children whom I had befriended in Israel. Most prominent was Gabi Mamson, the daughter of my mother's closest friend. But there were others who made the journey, like the Eisingers, whose daughter Roni I regularly saw at the gatherings.

How my father earned a living while we lived in Frankfurt is another mystery. In his video testimony, he mentions that he secured a job at "a plant for switchboard controls." That was a complete surprise to me when I saw the recording. My only connection to his work at the time was tangible evidence seared in my memory, which involved the regular arrival of sturdy brown cardboard boxes containing what I understood to be laundry detergent, possibly containing bleach, packed into plastic jars.

In reassembling disconnected snippets of memory, I believe that while in France, the brothers Gronner had agreed to use Rudy's experience and connections in the laundry business to expand distribution of cleaning products in Germany. I distinctly recall business cards my father had printed for a firm called *HADEFRA*, a German acronym for German-French trading agency. The other brand name that has stuck is *Droga Weiss*, alliterating the word for drugs and whiteness.

When I relate this recollection to my children and nephews now, it elicits guffaws that their grandfather was potentially a drug dealer. But I know that not to be the case, because the pungent substance definitely smelled like cleaning products.

Believing that my father was just a budding entrepreneur, at age ten or so I had no inkling how he would leverage our presence in Frankfurt to commence his legal fight for restitution. The first compensation was almost immediate, he recalled years later, when our family arrived in Frankfurt claiming returnee status. Under postwar West German law, former Jewish citizens who left Nazi Germany and returned were eligible for compensation of six thousand marks each for themselves and their children.

I didn't know at the time about my father's collaboration with Rudy to seriously pursue restitution compensation that the International Claims Commission had established for a variety of injustices perpetrated during the Nazi years. Now aware of the bureaucratic obstacles involved, I can only imagine the time they spent researching, engaging lawyers, filling out forms and submitting documentation to substantiate their claims for restitution.

AFTER LEAVING THE PENSION, we had two subsequent addresses, but I only remember the second—a newly constructed apartment building at 54 am Tiergarten. As its name connotes, it was in back of the Frankfurt Zoo, and the odors of animal waste and hay feed drifted into our apartment windows over the brick wall that ringed it.

If there is a more compelling explanation for my sketchy recall of life living in Frankfurt, I would say it was my school experience. Were it not for class photos, I would be unable to remember anything—and even as I study the images, I can't name the teacher, or any of the other boys. The lone, vivid remembrance is from my biology class, where it is an understatement to say I felt like a fish out of water—or in this instance— waterfowl. I remember being on the verge of tears with frustration when my native German classmates could easily recite the names of bird species, leaving me clueless. The best I could muster is *Ente* for duck and *Schwan* for swan. To this day I can't cite the German name for sparrow or canary—let alone any varieties of the species!

The feeling of isolation was reinforced when my classmates attended religious instruction on certain school days. As the lone Jewish kid in the class, I was excused from this otherwise mandatory course because my parents had enrolled me in Sunday school at the Jewish Community Center. I was literally segregated, and so traumatized that I have no recollection of how I spent that time. My parents also enrolled me in Jewish overnight camps that I attended in Germany. Photos show me with a group of boys, outwardly expressing the joy of spending summertime in the country. Yet I cannot unearth a single name or event from those summers. It is a complete void.

A SIDE BENEFIT OF HAVING GERMAN CITIZENSHIP reinstated was the advantage it gave my father's family in the competitive quest for an immigration visa to the United States. American authorities had set higher immigration quotas for post-war Europeans than for those from other regions: Jeckes who had returned to Germany improved their odds of success of being admitted to the United States, as compared to people applying from Israel. And, in my father's calculation, pocketing twenty-five thousand Deutschmarks was a way to finance the journey.

We benefited from what Donald Trump has derided as chain migration—the long-admired policy that has promoted immigration to unite families. It was the reason my Opa Moshe and Oma Leah came to Frankfurt, subsequently leaving when they obtained visas to join Mady and Kuba in the Bronx. At about the same time, their daughter—my aunt Esther—joined by her husband, and their children, left Tel Aviv, also settling in the Bronx.

By 1959, my friend Gabi and her family left Germany for America, as had the Eisingers. For a long time, I hoped we would leave Germany to go home. But after two years abroad, "home" was a fading notion in my consciousness. I was no longer in touch with the Holon friends I had left behind, and those whom I was regularly seeing in Germany were leaving for America. I had become an itinerant with no roots.

But as long as I was with my parents and sister, I felt at home. It's what I learned much later about how my mother had coped with the disruption she encountered when she was left behind in Germany as her family left for Palestine, and later in coming to America.

Interviewed for the Shoah Foundation oral history project in 1996, she was repeatedly asked how it felt to be reunited with her parents in Haifa, and, again many years later in New York. "I felt at home," she stated simply in both cases.

WITH HIS GERMAN IDENTITY as Joachim Heinz Gronner officially restored in a newly issued passport from the Federal Republic of Germany, my father now turned to our U.S. resident family for help in applying for immigration papers. To assist in this quest, a longtime friend of my Opa Moshe from Berlin, now living in Brooklyn, was recruited to sign an affidavit on my family's behalf. The name Leo Meissner would emerge decades later in a twist of fate worthy of mention in this family saga.

Were it not for a photo documenting our farewell in Rotterdam, I would not remember that Onkel Rudy, Tante Lydie and Jean-Luc had come to see us off. Studying my sad expression, I can only conclude I was not thrilled by the idea of again boarding a ship bound for another country. I had noted the date in the childhood photo album my mother had begun when I was born. It was now one day before my twelfth birthday, September 14, 1959.

CHAPTER 13

Becoming American

CROSSING THE ATLANTIC on the Holland-America Line's *S.S. Maasdam* led me to swear off ocean liner cruising for years—at least until I ventured on an Inside Passage cruise after a memorable trip to Alaska some four and a half decades later.

My seasickness began as early as the English Channel leg to Ireland and resumed pretty much for the entire interminable transatlantic crossing. The only relief I found was time spent in the fresh sea air of the upper deck, dreading the bunk several decks below in a tiny cabin I shared with my family. Although the ship's crew had prepared a special meal for my birthday, I don't recall eating it for fear of heaving it up. From my perch, the sight of the south shore of Long Island was a most welcome relief, because I knew we would soon arrive in New York.

Actually, we berthed in what I later learned was Hoboken, New Jersey, from where Esther's husband—my uncle Peppe—drove us into the longest tunnel I had ever encountered. Before long, we arrived in what became a virtual family compound in the West Bronx—relatives who lived in buildings literally across the street from one another on the same block.

The four of us encamped with the designated kin: Aba and Ima were assigned to stay with Opa and Oma, my mother's parents; I was deposited up the block with Esther's family, reconnecting with my familiar cousins Yair and Dorith from Tel Aviv; and Tami was across the street, sharing the bedroom of our cousins Daphne and Leslie, both of whom we were just meeting for the first time.

It being September, coinciding with a new academic year, my highly organized (and presumably well-informed and connected) aunt Mady had already laid out plans for me to attend the seventh grade at Macombs Junior High School 82 on University Avenue, where Daphne had just begun the eighth grade. Not only would we go to the same school, she explained, we would have the same homeroom assigned to all members of school orchestra class, where Daphne was studying the violin. Mady's lobbying on my behalf to be in the orchestra class was based on a misconception that I had studied the flute in Israel.

In fact, when I arrived for school I was handed my assigned flute, an instrument that I did not play, and then tried to explain that I had actually studied music on the recorder. "Flute like zis, not like zis," I said, gesturing the difference in how each instrument is played.

"Oh, this is the only kind of flute we teach here," the teacher said.

The issue of staying in Daphne's homeroom turned moot in any case: I needed to be placed in a remedial class until my language skills improved. My newly assigned seventh-grade class consisted of academically challenged students like Mario, a sixteen-year-old with facial hair so dense and dark that he could barely hide it even with the closest shave. Many years later, I looked back in fondness when the television show *Welcome Back, Kotter* featured a remedial class of "sweathogs"—seemingly modeled after mine.

Still, I credit the New York City public schools and an immensely dedicated veteran teacher with silver-blue hair, Miss Brennan, for helping me improve my English skills within three months, enough to qualify for transfer to the regular seventh- grade track.

My industrious father, fluent in English yet prone to come up with British terms or pronunciation unfamiliar to Americans, was able to secure a machine tool sales position in fairly quick order, enabling us to afford a fourth-story walkup apartment on University Avenue. We lived in cramped quarters, with Tami and me sharing the small bedroom, and my parents spending nights on a convertible sofa in the living room. The apartment was within easy walking distance to school, and slowly but surely I adapted to my new American surroundings and classmates.

It's hard to imagine now, but in today's parlance I would have been referred to as an "inner city" kid. Our bedroom window opened on a fire escape above University Avenue, meaning that the street below was the major interstate truck thoroughfare between Florida and Maine— U.S. Route 1. The noise went on incessantly and was especially severe on hot nights when we had to keep the window open.

Thankfully, my father learned to navigate the available social services for the underprivileged, and I was able to get out of town by spending three weeks at Surprise Lake Camp, a beneficiary of the United Jewish Appeal-Federation of Jewish Philanthropies. It was a memorable respite in the New York exurbs, and living in a tent in the country setting felt like worlds away. The experience was also a means to accelerate my Americanization.

TELEVISION BECAME A KEY VEHICLE for my American acculturation. There had been no television during my time in Israel, and we did not own a TV in the two years we lived in Frankfurt. Still, thanks to kind neighbors, my sister and I were invited to watch some evening programs at their apartment.

But once my parents secured our own apartment in the Bronx, my father took the first step toward middle-class life by buying us the first black-and-white television. After school, I thoroughly enjoyed watching the easy-to-comprehend slapstick fare of *The Three Stooges*.

I was soon attracted to the innovative commercials of the early Sixties, which helped me begin to appreciate new figures of speech, ironic phrases, nuances, and *double-entendres* in the English language. The industry paper *Advertising Age* has referred to this period as the "creative revolution," later depicted in the iconic *Mad Men* television series. This initial exposure to the power of language eventually matured into my future vocational interest in writing and communication.

IN ALL MY YEARS GROWING UP, I do not recall ever attending religious services with my parents. The sole Jewish ritual regularly practiced in my home was the Friday night candle lighting and *Kiddush* led by my otherwise non-observant father. It was my grandfather Moshe who regularly attended worship, and as his first-born grandson, he often called upon me to accompany him to the little orthodox *shul* one block down the Burnside Avenue hill.

I recall one particular *Simchat Torah* holiday, a festive event marking the last weekly Torah reading of the year and commencement of a new cycle beginning with the Book of Genesis. This joyous occasion spawned a tradition of unknown origin that called for alcohol consumption. My inebriated grandfather, joining other congregants, danced around the pews and managed to stuff a pinch of snuff up my nostrils. I didn't like it and now recognize the act as physical abuse.

Opa Moshe was the Bakel family patriarch, and for as long as I remember it was he who had led the annual Passover *seder*, where attendance was mandatory. The tradition seamlessly was transferred from Tel Aviv to the Bronx after the Bakel clan resettled in America.

As I approached the year of becoming a bar mitzvah, it was inevitable that I would need to prepare for the big event by studying my Torah portion, titled *Netzavim Vayelech*, a segment from Deuteronomy that is traditionally read on the Sabbath immediately preceding Rosh Hashanah.

My parents joined the Hebrew Institute of University Heights, and I studied with a tutor to learn the musical trope I would need to chant my Torah portion and the *Haftarah,* the supplementary reading drawn from the prophet Isaiah. Being part of the post-war baby boom, the synagogue's crowded bar mitzvah calendar forced me to share the date with three or four other boys who would be called to read scripture on the same day. I had a leg up on every one of them, since my native Hebrew reading skills were far superior to theirs.

By the time of my bar mitzvah in 1960, my father had become a sales engineer for Simplex Machinery Corporation, a metalworking-machine vendor based, among numerous such companies, along Centre and Grand Streets in lower Manhattan, then in the shadow of New York City police headquarters.

My guess is that, in his desire to spare me embarrassment, my father had asked his colleague Ben Roberts, a former teacher, to rephrase the rudimentary words I had struggled to compose into remarks I would deliver on the day I would be accepted into manhood by my fellow Jewish tribesmen. For the benefit of some of the other resettled Israelis whom my parents had invited, Aba had written a supplementary Hebrew greeting for me, recognizing that even though my English was not yet up to snuff, my fourth-grade-level Hebrew fluency was already beginning to fade.

I recall that many of my parents' *Jecke* friends later congregated in the living room of our apartment. Among them were our Holon neighbors—the Mamson family. Pico had brought a bulky reel-to-reel tape recorder into the bedroom in order to capture for posterity the words I had read in the synagogue. I still have the audio recording of my awkward tripping over Ben Roberts' words in an accented teenage voice that is barely audible above the din from the crowd assembled in our living room.

With the approach of fall, my Americanized aunt Mady, well versed in the mores of the country she had lived in for the past decade, briefed us on the unfamiliar holiday called Thanksgiving. Under her tutelage, we celebrated our first Thanksgiving feast in America at the Howard Johnson's restaurant on Fordham Road, where we were told Americans dined on the turkey special while wearing their best holiday outfits.

I ENCOUNTERED AN EPIC PERFECT STORM of emotional distress over the next two years. I was dealing simultaneously with the onset of adolescence and the difficulty of penetrating cliques of pubescent boys and girls who had known each other since primary school.

One solution was to link up with the few Israeli kids in my school. The Schnitzer cousins come to mind. Through them I found a neighborhood falafel joint that served as an after-school hangout, where we spent countless hours ruminating about our new lives, our aspirations—and mostly about the hottest girls. Some years later, *Saturday Night Live* seemed to satirize our experiences in the recurring appearance of the "Wild and Crazy Guys." Steve Martin and Dan Aykroyd portrayed a pair of maladjusted immigrants awkwardly attempting to adapt to American culture.

My Hebrew given name had become an albatross that hindered my own socialization. I became a target of taunts that twisted the name Amnon into a variety of pronunciations like Armand and Onion. Some used the contraction for "I'm going to," with taunts like "Ammana beat you up", which they followed with derisive guffaws. Once, when I was a student monitor, a boy said that to me before kicking me in the groin when I told him to wait on a landing to let another class pass by.

From my current perspective, this kind of sophomoric behavior would be recognized as bullying, not unlike the kind my father had encountered in Ilmenau. Though he had grown up alongside his schoolmates, they had fallen under the spell of the Nazi ideology that was reinforced by their parents—that he was not really German because he was Jewish.

Similarly, because of my foreign name and accent, I was treated differently from the native born kids. One way I confronted the problem was to introduce myself simply as "Sam," the middle name I had been given in memory of my grandfather. With the passage of time, I absorbed the patois of my Bronx neighborhood and morphed into just another guy named Sam. "My name is Sam." What could be more American than having the same name as America's iconic uncle? By 1965, my naturalization document formalized the name change.

WITHIN TWO YEARS OF ARRIVING IN AMERICA, my father's success as sales engineer for Simplex enabled us to move to larger quarters in the same complex where my aunt Mady had been living with Kuba, Daphne, and Leslie. The building consisted of seven sections, each with an elevator. The central courtyard, with somewhat unkempt plantings, was past its days of pre-war glory. Yet the imposing edifice still provided an air of pretense that made the complex at 1950 Andrews Avenue stand out in the neighborhood.

We were now smack dab in the virtual family compound. Visiting my cousin Daphne meant descending by elevator, walking across the lobby, and catching another elevator up. My younger cousins Yair and Dorith lived in the corner building at 1944 Andrews. My grandparents' apartment stood across 179th Street, sharing the same address as my father's aunt Rose, her husband Leo Selinger, and their son Fred.

The Erbers, my parents' friends from Holon, with their daughters Aliza and Varda, also lived in our complex.

The new apartment allowed my parents to have their own bedroom apart from the living room, but I had to share the second bedroom with my sister. The solution was a flimsy room divider made of laminated whiteboards, in frames affixed by spring-loaded posts stretching from floor to ceiling.

Upon completing eighth grade, I commuted by subway to the all-boys DeWitt Clinton High School.

When it came to choosing foreign language instruction, I could easily have excelled in Hebrew, like some of the Israeli classmates I had met in high school. Instead, likely because of my family connection, I chose to study French. I immediately excelled in the subject, and it became the fourth addition in my linguistic toolbox.

Recalling his own 1935 French summer immersion in Paris, my father arranged for me to spend the school vacation between my sophomore and junior year with his brother's family. By then, Onkel Rudy has become the Benelux sales representative for a welding equipment firm, and the family had moved to Brussels, Belgium. Moreover, my aunt and uncle had bought a country home in northern France, where Tante Lydie and Jean-Luc would spend the summer, with Onkel Rudy regularly coming from Brussels for extended weekends.

I had totally forgotten that I kept a journal of that vacation until I located it as part of the groundwork for this memoir. It is quite a revelation to read the almost-daily entries that begin on July 7 and run through September 3, 1963.

Almost from the start of the visit in Brussels, I noted my first negative impressions of my cousin, three years my junior. *Played cards. Jean-Luc cheats a lot. He is still very babyish,* I wrote. We spent the subsequent two weeks in Brussels getting reacquainted by playing tennis and sightseeing, but not really bonding.

The change of scene in Plachy, a hamlet in Picardie, made a favorable impression. *The house is very comfortable inside,* I noted, observing it was only one of four or five homes or farms. *I have a room all for myself with a large bed. From my window I can also see hills with green pastures and forests.*

I was put to work cutting hedges almost immediately after arrival, but then I noted in the journal: *Dug a hole for nothing because Jean-Luc said there are all kinds of ancient remnants here.* So in addition to cheating at games, he was up to practical jokes, I gathered.

Several days later, we set up an ad-hoc badminton net with a rope tied to some trees. *It seems to me it's impossible to play a decent game with Jean-Luc without getting mad.* Earlier that morning, I had noted, *He really got his mother mad. I didn't understand why.*

Later that day I was angry enough to write, *Today I had reason to run away from this place. Jean-Luc told me that until I came he wanted to see me very much, but that now he doesn't want me here anymore. He also added that I should do something about my French because this was probably the main reason I came here. I responded by saying that the main reason was to see him and his parents after three years. For that, he laughed in my face.*

I had kept clear of Jean-Luc over the ensuing days—even taking a walk by myself. I was at the age where my interests diverged from those of my pesky twelve-year-old cousin, and I took an interest in a group of girls I had encountered in my excursion around the village. I learned that they were dancers who would perform in the town fair. *I sure don't want to miss it,* I noted in my journal.

I was elated to see my uncle return from Brussels. *It seems that when Onkel Rudy is here, there is peace in the air for everyone,* I wrote. *It feels so great to have him around. I don't have this feeling with anyone except Aba. I guess that they are very much alike. I also like this uncle of mine like no other. . .almost like my own father.*

In fact, the morning following the town fair, my uncle took me aside after breakfast and asked me what was wrong. I related the sequence of events that had led Jean-Luc to say the hurtful things to me—which my cousin claimed he said only after I refused to play with him.

Uncle also told Jean-Luc it was one of the most impolite things one can do, to tell someone who came thousands of miles for a visit that he didn't want him here—even though he felt it.

Onkel Rudy's admonition was well handled. *All's forgotten and OK,* I later wrote, noting Jean-Luc and I had completed a sixteen-kilometer ride on our bikes. *I am happy again and I just hope that my stay will remain only one half as pleasant as it was today.*

In fact it did, as we went on more rides, played darts, and hiked, even though my uncle had left for Brussels.

On August 3 my journal entry reported that Onkel Rudy had again returned, but that Uncle Sylvain had also made the journey from Paris on his Peugeot 104 moped.

While Aunt Lydie and Onkel Rudy left to go shopping in Amiens, the large town nearest to Plachy, we spent time with my grandfather Sami's youngest brother. We strolled in the fields behind the house and played the uniquely French "boule" game, and threw darts. With ever-present cigarette smoke rising from the unfiltered *Gauloises* between his yellow index and middle fingers, Sylvain also regaled us with Jewish jokes, interspersed with a characteristic smokers' cough after each punchline.

The journal covers several weeks in the lives of three birds we tried to rescue after they had fallen out of a nest during a massive storm. In the end, they all died.

I had plenty of opportunity to practice my French, not only with Jean-Luc, but with my aunt, whom I had grown to adore. With much difficulty, we would engage in conversations on wide-ranging topics, covering family, the civil rights marches, and the environment.

I also got to meet some of the farmers' kids in the village, some who bestowed on me the nickname "Le Ricain," short for "l'Americain." How odd, I thought, that less than four years after arriving in New York, some kids in the French countryside regarded as me as a Yankee, while back home I was still ambivalent about my national identity.

READING THE JOURNAL REMINDED ME that my summer visit with the Gronner branch was followed by a short stay with my maternal uncle Shimshon, who by then had left Kibbutz Ramat Yochanan to take an assignment as head of Israel Bonds in Europe. Along with my aunt Dvora and two of their girls, they were living in Frankfurt.

My journal includes this entry for August 25, describing my departure from the Amiens train station:

> Aunt Lydie gave me a couple of sandwiches. She said the food on the train is no good and very expensive. When we left, I couldn't hold my tears back. Who knows when I'll see them again?

I switched trains in Paris and arrived in Frankfurt late in the evening, greeted by the family. *Everyone got older and the girls are real young ladies now. Tirza is about my height*, I noted.

Over the course of my stay, traveling around town by streetcar, the veil that had obscured my recollections of Frankfurt began to recede, revealing colorized versions of landmarks I remembered only as dull sepia or gray images. Here was Melemstrasse, one of the places where we had lived, and I noted the name of the school I attended, Helmholtzschule. The notes in my journal helped revive names of familiar destinations like the Kaufhof department store, and the main shopping avenue called Zeil and the major streetcar intersection at Hauptwache.

My journal indicates that I had left Frankfurt by plane on September 2, landing in Paris and spending one night in a hotel room near Uncle Sylvain. The following day it was back to the airport and the flight home with a change of planes in Amsterdam.

Home. I realized then that America had become home for me.

CHAPTER 14

Finding Direction

Academically, I excelled at DeWitt Clinton High School. On the basis of my grades, I was assigned to several honors classes, where I befriended guys whose trajectory would lead them to the most prestigious colleges.

Unlike those native English speakers, though, I felt challenged on the standard language skills examinations; I did not read as fast as they did, and it took me longer to process words to comprehend the content and context of what I was reading. To address this handicap, my parents signed me up for a speed-reading course that I attended for a while on Saturday mornings. It helped somewhat but did little to sufficiently calm my nerves whenever it was time to take the SAT for college qualification. Even the math portion of the examination was a challenge, as many of the problems posed were in verbal form, requiring careful reading of the question.

Another disadvantage I faced was my family's unfamiliarity with the secret of navigating the college guidance office and possibility of obtaining financial aid. There appeared to be a pecking order with classification of student tiers, under which the students in the Scholarship School were deemed more academically ready for reputable private universities even than those, like me, who had been tagged for the Honor School. I shared many courses with Scholarship students, but they appeared to have an inside track with the College Placement Office.

My father had intimated that affordability should be a primary concern in my college selection. In response, the placement office steered me toward publicly supported colleges over private universities. Among the recommendations, I was drawn to Harpur College in Binghamton, part of the State University of New York. My stereotypical image of American campus life in a distant college town was a big draw.

But Aba had a different idea. His reservation about this path was likely influenced by his own early interest in machinery, which had led him to resolve to pursue a career in engineering. In contrast, even at seventeen, I had not settled on any trajectory leading to a financially secure career in engineering, medicine, law, or business. My interest in high school was in the humanities and the arts—specifically performance art.

From the outset as a freshman at DeWitt Clinton, I signed up for the drama club, which led me to be assigned to a special homeroom class designated as Squad A. The planned performance that year was ideal for an all-boys school because the play—*Stalag 17*—had no female characters. I won the role of Sergeant Schultz, a smaller part that called for me to recite lines in a heavy German accent, for which I naturally was a shoo-in.

The camaraderie of my Squad A cohort was palpable and a striking contrast to my American initiation in junior high school. I was accepted as a peer, not regarded as some awkward new kid with a strange foreign name. I relished the praise, winning another part in the play *Blood, Sweat and Stanley Poole*, which called for me to play the role of Angelo Bucci with a heavy Italian-American accent. I appeared in other productions, most notably playing Scrooge, the lead role in *A Christmas Carol*.

For a period of time, I commuted to midtown Manhattan to be part of a small theater company especially designed for New York high school students. Having been accepted by audition, the training consisted of workshops incorporating music and dance that, together, were being developed for an off-off Broadway production entitled *If We Grow Up*. As the performance date approached, the after-school rehearsals became more frequent, causing me to fall behind in my homework. My parents intervened and convinced me to drop out of the program.

I SAT DOWN WITH MY PARENTS for a family discussion after I received my acceptance notice from Harpur College.

"This is wonderful news and we are very proud," my father said. "But please consider another option. Ima and I have been discussing moving out of the Bronx into our own house in the suburbs. We certainly want you to attend college, but if you go out of town, we will not be able to afford both. Your grade point average qualifies you for City College, which charges no tuition. If you go to CCNY, you will be able to get your degree and we will be able to buy a house."

I did not immediately understand my father's logic. On reflection, Aba likely calculated that, with no clear career choice, why spend money unnecessarily when his son could get a free education at a college with a reputation for helping immigrants enter the middle class? After all, CCNY is the gateway to the streets that are paved with gold, he reasoned.

Would he have felt otherwise if I had let him know that I wanted to become a doctor? Or lawyer? Or engineer like him?

This turned out to be an academic inquiry. The theoretical choice he put before me was illusory, because he knew I could not countenance the thought that it was I who had prevented my parents from living their ideal American life in the suburbs.

What I saw at work was the emergence of my father's negotiating skills, which would lead him to become a successful entrepreneur. He essentially disarmed me and trivialized my idea of attending an out-of-town school, especially because I had no firm grasp on what I would want to do after I graduated.

Though it lacked residential halls, City College was actually the perfect commuter school choice for me. It had a rich history in the social sciences and humanities, and its chemistry, physics, and engineering programs had by then spawned a number of Nobel Laureates. From its founding in 1847 as the Free Academy of the City of New York, its mission has been to educate the immigrant and working class as a means toward upward mobility.

But there was a hitch. Free tuition only applied to New York City resident high school graduates. Non-resident tuition was four hundred dollars for each academic year on top of administrative student fees amounting to around fifty dollars.

It was there that I saw my father revive an insurrectional streak I had first witnessed years earlier in Naples, when I helped him smuggle the cigarettes off the ship. If he could find a way around restrictive rules and regulations, he had no qualms about circumventing them as a means to an end. Was this attitude formed in Germany, where perverse edicts and regulations were legally imposed to unjustly strip Jews of their assets? When the Jewish Agency successfully established clandestine means of saving Jewish refugees contrary to British restrictions on immigration, hadn't the means justified the end?

I don't know what drove my father to get me to falsify my application to City College by entering my residence as the address of my aunt Esther and uncle Peppe, who by then had purchased a home in the Whitestone section of Queens. But if he was motivated by frugality, it is hard to imagine that all this subterfuge had saved less than two thousand dollars from our family budget over my entire college career.

But the cost to my self-confidence was immeasurable. Throughout my undergraduate college years, I resorted to lies and deception to guard our family secret.

Like many students, I commuted to the uptown Manhattan campus by public transit. I first had to travel on an interstate bus from my parents' new home in Bergenfield, New Jersey. Once at the George Washington Bridge Bus Terminal, I walked down to Broadway and boarded the M100 bus that dropped me off on Amsterdam Avenue, on the western edge of the campus.

I cannot describe the daily trepidation of being seen emerging from M100 bus or running into someone I knew and having to answer a seemingly harmless question about my commute. Anyone who knows anything about New York City would know that commuting to the college from the borough of Queens means taking the subway, never a bus—and, least of the all the M100.

Conversely, I felt the need to keep up appearances with New Jersey acquaintances, lest inquiries open the can of worms about my free college education. I avoided wearing CCNY paraphernalia and even created the illusion that I commuted each day to New York University by affixing an NYU decal to the back window of my father's Plymouth Valiant.

With thousands of commuting students, I began to feel very isolated at City College—a sense made worse by my reluctance to really bond with anyone for fear of being found out as a freeloader.

That's why, in the fall of my second year I decided to undergo the indignity of pledging Tau Epsilon Phi fraternity. I chose them because unlike Alpha Epsilon Pi, it did not cater exclusively to Jewish students. The most attractive benefit to me was their house at the corner of Convent Avenue and 144th Street, which became a center of my social connections on campus. I regret that my TEP connections, as strongly as I felt them during my college years, were severed almost immediately after I completed my studies.

TO APPLY GENERAL MACARTHUR'S PHRASE about old soldiers, I faded away from my City College student experience and, though I earned my bachelors degree, I never actually attended the commencement. The transition from college to work life just happened organically, and I will forever be grateful to one man who made it happen: Professor Irving Rosenthal.

I first met Irving upon my return to CCNY's uptown campus following a depressing semester at the Baruch School, at the time the college's business administration facility at the intersection of Twenty-Third Street and Lexington Avenue. Its light brick façade and tall classroom windows reminded me of De Witt Clinton. The cavernous hallways reinforced this impression, especially when they filled with a stream of harried students emerging from classrooms at dismissal— many toting briefcases to or from their office jobs elsewhere in Manhattan.

I had mistakenly thought that I would pursue a degree in advertising, based solely on the *Mad Men* imagery I had conjured up about the creators of the television ads I had devoured when I came home from junior high school. I longed to be trapped in the creative dens of Madison Avenue as a copywriter, inventing engaging and memorable campaigns that employed jingles, plays on words, and double meanings.

"Well, advertising is not taught here," someone in the CCNY career guidance office uptown had informed me. "For that you have to transfer downtown to Baruch."

I had a rude awakening when I showed up for class. The advertising prerequisites included introductions to marketing concepts, statistics, and management. How is all this related to the creative part of the business? I asked myself. What is the purpose of learning about probability, when my statistics course instructor consistently chose to make a point by fishing a deck of cards out of his baggy trousers? I'd always hated games of chance—especially poker.

As a complete neophyte—dare I say ignoramus—I was still too immature to grasp the core business objectives behind successful ad campaigns. Besides, who wanted to go to school with accounting students who rushed off to work with those clumsy square briefcases? I had seen enough, given it a try, and resolved to go back uptown.

AFTER ACQUIRING THE HOUSE in the suburbs, my ambitious father had left Simplex, and from the family den, begun to leverage the connections and customer base he had built for the firm to launch his own machinery supply business. The former Israeli socialist labor activist was now a full-fledged capitalist entrepreneur who had a knack for skillfully combining his knowledge of machine tools and the craft of hardnosed negotiation into a winning formula. If this was a genetic trait passed down through Onkel Willi and Sami, it clearly ended with Aba, because neither of his children inherited it.

As Speedycut Company began to gain traction, my parents were not pleased with my listlessness. My father was beginning to churn the idea for a Plan B—that I might become his apprentice and, perhaps, eventually join him after I obtained my undergraduate degree.

It was the farthest thing from my mind. I was caught in a captive state of unrest, trapped within myself with no direction, cognizant of the swirl of student protests on campus against the America's involvement in Vietnam, and afraid that I would eventually be drafted into the military.

I LEAFED THROUGH THE CITY COLLEGE CATALOG as if it were a restaurant menu, looking for courses that would strike my fancy. My interest in a writing career had not waned, but I had put aside the notion of getting into the ad business.

The closest thing I found of possible interest was an introduction to journalism. Although part of the English Department, the curriculum would not lead to a degree, but, if paired with my declared major—Political Science—I saw it as a possible way into a respectable career in the news business.

Professor Rosenthal immediately enthralled me in his journalism course. He circulated shining examples of compelling newswriting that drew the reader into the article. I recall the first exercise he gave, listing a series of facts in random order that we were to turn into a compelling "lede"—shorthand for the opening paragraph of a news article.

I was immediately smitten with the class and especially with Rosenthal's inspirational teaching style, invoking names of past students who had taken the class and had since become luminaries in the field. He had started teaching in the 1930s, inspiring future journalists like A.M Rosenthal of *The New York Times*, Ed Kosner of *Esquire*, and Daniel Schorr of CBS and National Public Radio.

I would tell people years later that he had lit the spark in my belly too, and launched my career.

At about that time, my father gave me his Plymouth Valiant. I didn't like driving to school because it was hard to find a parking spot. In gratitude and feeling obliged, though, I did drive in if my father asked me to pick up machine tool parts from some of his suppliers on Centre Street.

When this got to be onerous, I initiated the discussion about his expectations. "Aba, I love you and want to help you, but I have no interest in becoming part of your business," I said. "Please don't rely on me for the errands, because I now know what I want to do, and it does not involve Speedycut."

"Very well," he answered, disappointment in his voice. "I am glad you have found a direction you want to pursue, and that makes me happy."

Not long afterward, he brought in a younger man, experienced in the field. Jeff Lafer would eventually become his partner and help the business grow from a rented garage to a large modern space in Fairfield, New Jersey.

In my first year with Professor Rosenthal, I happened to see a classified ad in the local New Jersey newspaper for what was described as a "news clerk." It was a part-time weekend position that suited my schedule. Les Barreaux, one of the main editors at the *Bergen Record*, conducted the job interview. Noting that I was studying journalism, he was taken back by my effusive enthusiasm about the job.

"Let me reset your expectations, Sam" he told me. "The main job description is to screen calls to the city desk, route them to the right department, and gather information from funeral homes to write obituaries."

I didn't care. As far as I was concerned, I had my foot in the door at a *real* daily newspaper, and I gloated about it in class at the first opportunity.

Finding Direction

In early 1969 Professor Rosenthal told the class about a summer reporting internship sponsored by The Newspaper Fund, the charitable arm of Dow Jones and Company and publisher of *The Wall Street Journal*. To qualify for the five-hundred-dollar stipend, I would need to work as a reporter, covering and writing news for a daily paper. He would gladly write the required faculty recommendation.

Having several months' experience and established connections, I appealed to my editors to allow me to become a reporting intern for the summer. The disappointing answer came from the Carl Jellinghaus, the executive editor: "Sam, you're doing a great job on the news desk, but we don't have a summer internship program."

I was devastated. Since becoming news clerk, I had been taken under the wing of one of the desk editors, John Lancelloti, who over time had handed me some press releases for simple rewrite. He also remembered that, on my own initiative, I had written a commentary for the Op-Ed page in response to a bulletin board posting soliciting replacement columns to fill in for the vacationing William A. Caldwell, the Pulitzer Prize-winning associate editor.

The notice was most assuredly meant for the reporters and editors—certainly not for the kid who was there to answer phones. But one day my mother told me someone had called from the paper looking for me. When I returned the call, I learned the column was running short and they needed me to fill in a couple of inches.

John felt terrible for me, but as my *de facto* mentor, he took it upon himself to call his former boss, Harry Anderson, the city editor at the *Newark Evening News*, to recommend me for the summer internship. I was hired immediately after my interview, and spent that summer in a vortex of the major metropolitan daily in New Jersey, earning my journalistic stripes from long-time, hardened reporters and editors.

CHAPTER 15

America Been Berry, Berry Good to Me

I N A SKETCH THAT AIRED on *Saturday Night Live on* November 8, 1978, comedian Garrett Morris introduced his recurring role as Chico Escuela, the immigrant Costa Rican baseball player and re-tired star for the Chicago Cubs. Ostensibly a guest speaker at a Knights of Columbus event, the *faux* Chico, in a heavy Spanish accent, limits his remarks to this:

Thank you berry much. Baseball been berry, berry good to me. Thank you. God bless you. Gracias!

In the context of my family's American experience, six decades long at this writing, Chico's now-familiar quote rings so aptly for summariz-ing my father's aspirations for himself and the descendants of his par-ents.

Speedycut Company flourished over the years, providing my parents a financially secure and comfortable lifestyle. After graduating from Bergenfield High School, Tami, who adopted "Tammy" as her Americanized moniker, was off to Boston and obtained her undergraduate degree in special education from Northeastern University.

"I built up the company to a nice-sized corporation; inasmuch as my son did not want to be a part of it, I took in junior partners—one ten years younger, the other twenty-two years younger—to have a continuity," my father recalled in his video for the Visual History Foundation. "Eventually I stepped back and let the others fill the gap."

Like any self-respecting American entrepreneur, my father and his accountants took advantage of every tax benefit permitted to enhance my parents' living standard. As the transplanted Israeli *Jeckes* were entering their proverbial Golden Years with an eye toward a Florida retirement, in 1973 they bought an apartment in Pembroke Pines.

"At that time I had nothing specific in mind other than having a lot of friends and customers who liked to play golf," my tennis-loving father told the interviewer. "Inasmuch as the business could write off that part of the investment for businesses purposes, I used that portion for the write-off, and we only took about two weeks out of the year to stay in Florida."

The summer of 1973 was also a major personal milestone for me— the year of my marriage to "the girl next door"—who literally lived in the apartment adjacent to mine in Hackensack, New Jersey.

I had moved there in the spring of 1972 with my friend Max, one of the immigrants in the pack of Israelis I had befriended at the falafel hangout in the Bronx. Max had also attended DeWitt Clinton, but we'd remained close after his family moved to Spring Valley, a suburb about a thirty-minute drive north of the Bronx. He eventually graduated with a degree in education from the state university in New Paltz.

Upon completing my *Newark Evening News* internship, I attended evening classes at City College to earn my bachelor's degree in January

1970. I had moved out of my parents' home to Newark, subletting a studio apartment from a colleague who was temporarily in Boston attending Harvard University on a Nieman Fellowship.

I was enjoying my independence and budding journalism career, but only months later the Scudder family sold the money-losing, privately held daily and their profitable paper recycling plant to Media General, a Virginia-based conglomerate. This move precipitated an organizing drive to elect the Newspaper Guild as our union representative.

A summer-long strike ensued, and, unable to pay my rent from the weekly strike pay of thirty-five dollars, I reluctantly moved back to my parents' home. I spent countless hours scouring the trade magazine *Editor & Publisher* and responding to job listings across the country. I looked forward to picket duty just to break the routine, even though it meant picketing in front of the newspaper building in the sweltering summer heat. With plenty of free time at my disposal, I sat down to write about my daily routine. It felt good to see my byline in print again when *The Record* agreed to run the piece I had written as a commentary under the headline "Waiting for the Brush-Off."

By the fall of 1971 the new *Newark News* management and the Guild reached a settlement that called for the termination of some editorial staff in reverse order of seniority—and as one of the last hired, I was let go. I qualified for unemployment benefits and headed out of town to Killington, Vermont, where in prior years I had befriended the owner of a ski lodge. In return for room and board, I served breakfast, straightened out the dorm rooms and cleaned bathrooms. But I was free to spend plenty of time on the slopes.

With a new crop of weekly guests, I had the time of my life that winter, especially meeting a new contingent of women skiers each week. But in January, my mother called to advise me that someone from

United Press International had called looking for me.

I accepted a position in UPI's Newark bureau but discovered that the once-prominent wire service had declined into a shoestring operation. After only three days, I was expected to adeptly become a one-man bureau responsible for a myriad of duties: filing at least one hourly radio news script, fetching the mail and reporting deadline-driven news items, reporting a local angle for a national wire story, even taking calls from radio station clients to retransmit an earlier script that had been garbled in their Teletype printer.

My solo flight that first Saturday was a complete disaster, causing me to break down in a panic attack. Within weeks, UPI and I had a mutual parting of the ways. But it did not take long for me to land a job with the *Elizabeth Journal*, which assigned me to its Plainfield bureau in Union County. The daily commute was long, but compared to my UPI experience the workload was a breeze.

At about the same time, Max had landed a teaching position in a Rockland County school district just north of the New York state line. Like me, he was ready to move out of his parents' home. I proposed that we find a mid-point between our workplaces, and we settled on Hackensack.

On the day of our move the following March, Max discovered that our apartment adjoined one occupied by three women similar in age to us—Lauren, Karen and Irene. At some point, raven-haired Lauren and I went out on a date. But it was her blonde roommate Karen to whom I was attracted, and we became a couple over the ensuing months.

My budding relationship with Karen survived the odd arrangement of our work shifts—she and her roommate Irene commuted to their jobs at Roosevelt Hospital in Manhattan early in the morning, while I worked afternoons late into the night. Much of our courtship involved little ditties and notes I scribbled and slipped under her door when I came home in the wee hours. When her roommates weren't home, Karen spent many an evening with Max—a means to avoid being alone with Pyewacket, Lauren's hyperactive, champagne-colored Turkish Angora cat.

Our lives crisscrossed like ships across a vast ocean, with brief weekend encounters. The tedium of the long daily commute was wearing me down. Moreover, working in the Plainfield outpost of the *Elizabeth Journal*—far from the paper's nerve center in city room—led me to rethink my career path.

About then, our neighbors' one-year lease was close to expiring. Irene decided to move in with her boyfriend. Lauren was set to lease a place of her own. "Why don't you come live with me and Max?" I asked Karen when I heard the news, realizing she would need new housing. She agreed.

I had carried a grudge against the *Bergen Record* for rejecting my request for a paid reporting internship, but I resolved to swallow my pride and apply for a reporting job that would keep me closer to home.

I had by then amassed the reporting experience to qualify for a staff reporter position to cover several towns in Bergen County, minutes from our apartment. Since most town meetings took place in the evening, my hours still did not coincide with Karen's, but I would at least be able to come home to share dinner with her. The job offer was extended, and I agreed to start after my return from a planned vacation.

KAREN AND I DECIDED TO VISIT ISRAEL. I had not been back in fifteen years since leaving with my family, and we plotted an itinerary that would include a drive to the areas of the West Bank that had been under Jordanian control prior to 1967.

If ever there was a test of a relationship, the events that unfolded provided ample proof of the strength of our commitment to one another. In our exploration of the Arab villages that dotted the area, I stopped around lunchtime at a local grocery, where I bought us drinks, along with bread and cheese. The cheese came wrapped in newsprint, and Karen, a medical assistant, warned me against consuming it.

"The locals eat this, so why should I worry?" I commented. "I mean, how much worse could this be than buying a hot dog that's been stewing for hours in the Sabrett cart outside the bus terminal in Manhattan?" As I proceeded to eat, she reluctantly tasted it, grimacing and shaking her head.

She was right: Within hours, after returning to Jerusalem, we were both convulsed with severe stomach pains, and we fell into delirium from fever. We were staying with my mother's cousin and her husband, and they immediately took us to Hadassah Hospital. Under the effects of scorching fever and massive doses of opiates, I feared we would both die. I recall screaming, my voice mingling with that of a man on a gurney near mine who kept blurting out, "Doctor! Doctor!" in an incessant, re-petitive chorus throughout the night.

When it was over, and I came to my senses, I knew that I could not bear the thought of losing Karen. From the fear in her eyes, I surmised she felt likewise. We had survived a life-threatening challenge, and I knew that my love for her was a bond that I would never dissever.

FOR SEVERAL WEEKS AFTER the nightmare vacation, I ruminated about what had happened, thankful that Karen was sticking by me despite my attempt to kill both of us by food poisoning—and especially in defying her warning. This fealty served to convince me that she loved me.

One particular evening, when Max was not at home, I opened the conversation. "So, do you know that big temple on Summit Avenue, the one with the stained glass windows?"

"Yeah, we've passed it many times. What about it?"

"What if we got married there?"

Not very romantic, I admit. Rather practical, though, given that I was on dinner break and had to go out again to cover a story. I don't remember her immediately saying "yes" on the spot. But we did set up a meeting with the rabbi and set a date for July 1, 1973.

The first step was to meet the future in-laws, meaning driving to an area of Brooklyn I had never been to. We made our way to the Belt Parkway past Cropsey Avenue, an exit I remembered from an earlier trip to Coney Island with my Israeli kibbutz cousins who were on a visit to America. Driving further east along the shore of the Long Island Sound, I exited northward at Flatbush Avenue. A couple of turns later and we found ourselves in Mill Basin, a planned development of postwar single-family homes with front lawns—shattering my preconceived notion of Brooklyn housing stock.

I looked around as I parked the car, noticing that the Cadillac in the driveway across the street had an unusual feature at the time: a personalized vanity license plate.

Karen's mother, Jean Widder, greeted me at the door.

"What a lovely neighborhood, so different from what I had imagined," I said to break the ice. "Very impressive, especially the Caddy across the street with that GSM name plate."

"Oh, that one? That belongs to our friends George and Beverly Meissner," she responded.

"Meissner? Any relation to Leo Meissner?"

"Why, yes—Leo and Ida are George's parents."

I had heard of the term "Jewish geography" to describe the phenomenon of how Jews from various walks of life are connected to one another. In the broader world, it is generally described as six degrees of separation, popularized after a play about a fraudster who invokes names of people connected to his "mark" in order to fool them.

In this case, I had a first-degree connection to Leo and Ida, whom I knew as "Ita." I had met them numerous times in family gatherings involving my maternal grandparents, who had been good friends of theirs in Berlin. I did not know they had a son, George, much less that he and his wife lived across the street from the woman I was about to marry.

When I later revealed this coincidence to my parents, Aba told me that, if it hadn't been for Leo's affidavit, we would not have been able to immigrate to America. Moreover, Karen revealed that, for some time, on visits to Mill Basin, Ida had handed her slips of paper with names and phone numbers of "nice Jewish boys" that she would like.

When a Jewish grandmother tries to play the role of *shadchan*, you gratefully accept the information but then discard the note at the first opportunity: That is just what Karen did every time, without even looking at the note. But she now admitted that it is quite likely my name was among those that Ida had slipped her.

Was our pending nuptial *bashert*, as a Yiddish matchmaker would claim? It is still hard to resist the temptation to acknowledge that the mutual connection to the Meissners shared by Karen's family and mine was pre-ordained.

My parents invited the elder Meissners to our wedding, and Karen's parents, Jean and Paul, naturally asked Beverly and George to be their guests.

Our relatively short engagement came at a price: When we invited my only living grandparents to the wedding, we promised to drive them to the bungalow they had reserved the previous summer. That's how Karen and I came to spend our honeymoon with my Opa and Oma in the *Jecke*-influenced hamlet of Fleischmann's, New York.

CHAPTER 16

The Tree Flourishes

I HAD BEEN WORKING MY AFTERNOON and night shifts at *The Record* for about two years when we learned that Karen was pregnant with our first child. I asked my editors if I could transfer elsewhere on the staff when the baby arrived, but I was denied the request.

Faced with a career versus work life dilemma, I reached out to Professor Irving Rosenthal, my journalism mentor. I had remained in touch with him after he founded a professional affiliate of the City College Alumni Association devoted to graduates who were engaged in the field of communications—not merely journalism, but related specialties like broadcast news, public relations, public affairs, and advertising.

"Irving, I'll always be grateful to you for steering me and helping me get my start in news reporting," I said when we spoke by phone. "I love what I've done over the past five years, but now that I'm going to be a father, I want to spend my evenings at home. Is it a sell-out to become a flack?" I intentionally used a derogatory term that journalists employ to describe publicists.

"Absolutely not," he said. "PR is an honorable profession and is often indispensable to working reporters. Having been a reporter yourself, you know how a good PR person can locate leads and information on deadline, or even provide an expert to be interviewed. It's an honest living, and if it better fits you, go for it."

I followed through on his advice and began to peruse the jobs listings in *The New York Times* classified section.

As someone who matured in the Sixties, I reflected my generation's anti-corporate, anti-establishment bias. I had pursued journalism because it was a practical complement to my degree in political science. I enjoyed writing about substantive matters—local issues that affected my readers' lives or engaging features about their neighbors. If I were to become a propagandist, I ruled out becoming a spokesman for the military industrial complex.

Landing a job at the Anti-Defamation League national headquarters was the ideal solution to my predicament. I would be able to apply my writing experience to promote values I personally possessed—denouncing anti-Semitism and promoting civil rights for all minorities. When I told Irving where I had landed, he was elated.

The immediate personal benefit of my new job was being home with Karen. In the five years since leaving school, it was my first regular daytime job. It offered an additional benefit: Not having to work on any Jewish holidays—even minor ones.

KAREN AND HER PARENTS HAD THEIR FIRST CHANCE to meet Rudy and Lydie in the spring of 1974. My aunt and uncle had come to stay with my parents in advance of a planned cross-country trip by the foursome. Aba made a point of driving Rudy and Lydie to meet the new in-laws, Jean and Paul, in Brooklyn, as if to underscore to his older sibling that despite the losses they had suffered, the family was being reconstituted in the New World.

Lydie's limited ability to speak English did not inhibit communication, and everyone got along famously. To this day Karen recalls how the four Gronners had driven across America in my father's black Chrysler Imperial: "It's a Mafia car," she had joked, and Lydie had responded with hearty laughter.

No one was laughing several weeks later when Uncle Rudy had to spend a night in a jail cell in Bakersfield, California. Having shared driving duties with Aba, and unaccustomed to the smooth riding full sized American vehicle, Rudy had been pulled over by a highway patrolman on a desolate stretch of highway.

"Do you know how fast you were going?" the officer had asked.

"Were we speeding?" my father had intervened from the front passenger seat, having just been jolted from slumber.

"I clocked you at one hundred and ten," the cop had said. "This speed above the posted limit results in an immediate arrest. Please step out of the vehicle, sir."

My confused uncle had complied yet protested to my father that the speedometer had not moved much past one hundred.

"That may be so, but this speedometer is set to *miles* per hour," my father said in German.

"*Mon dieu!*" Rudy had exclaimed for Lydie's benefit, realizing that he was conditioned to the speedometer reading one-hundred-ten *kilometers* per hour, equivalent to only sixty-eight MPH.

The law being the law, Rudy had spent the night in lockup and was released with a warning after a brief court hearing the following day.

KNOWING WE WOULD NEED MORE ROOM once our baby arrived, Karen and I scoured our neighborhood and found a lovely larger space on the ground floor of a two-family private house on a quiet tree-lined street in Hackensack. After Arielle was born on October 20, 1974, we settled into an idyllic suburban life. The home with a bright south-facing living room, was a short walk from the train station, and Karen would often stroll over with the baby carriage and meet me at the end of the day.

Yet, as is often the case, though we were filled with optimism, fate intervened.

Through the latter part of the prior year, Karen had been consumed with tending to her brother Erik who was undergoing chemotherapy treatment at her workplace, Roosevelt Hospital. He had been diagnosed with Hodgkin's disease within weeks of our wedding, and she had helped secure Dr. Arthur Karanas as his oncologist. The strain on the family was palpable—the debilitating treatments, the risk of incurring infections, long trips from Brooklyn to Manhattan—had all taken a toll on Erik and her parents.

Erik's treatment was complicated by the presence of Gaucher's syndrome, a hereditary mutation commonly found in Ashkenazi families, which would prevent Dr. Karanas from pursuing the total body radiation called for in the normal Hodgkin's treatment protocol.

"WHAT'S WRONG?" I ASKED ONE DAY when I came home from work to find my spouse sitting on the living room couch, her feet on the plush white-and-brown Swedish rya rug we had recently bought as an initial investment.

"Erik will undergo a series of local radiation treatments to the nodes in his neck. I need to be close to my family," she announced. "I can't let my parents bring him to the hospital for radiation, and I can't be running back and forth to Brooklyn with the baby."

Almost immediately we moved with our infant daughter to a rental apartment on Avenue X in Brooklyn. I was gratified that Karen, who never earned a driver's license, was now able to travel by public bus and drop off our daughter at the Widders so she could accompany Erik on the trek to Manhattan for his radiation treatments. Being with Arielle was the best diversion for Jean in those days, doubly so whenever Karen's sister Lisa came to spend the day with her daughter Kate, a year older than Arielle. A double-dose of grandkids is twice as uplifting for any grandparent.

During this period, I watched Karen's parents rapidly compress years of aging into months. Erik coped exceptionally well. Although in a weakened state, he regularly managed to get to class at Brooklyn College. He reveled in his nieces, and, when he was up to it, he managed to play his saxophone in his room, often recording his practice sessions on a reel-to-reel tape recorder.

AT SOME POINT, AFTER A YEAR OF LIVING in an apartment that we both loathed, Karen and I discussed the option of buying a home. While on a visit to my parents one Sunday, she happened to glance through the *Bergen Record* real estate ads and spotted a house being offered for sale by an owner in Teaneck, the town adjoining Bergenfield to the south. We had already made the journey from Brooklyn and figured we had little to lose.

The wood-frame home was of early twentieth century vintage, featuring a covered front porch that had once wrapped around to the right, but since been modified to create a small den with a picture window facing the street.

At first glance, the house seemed barely serviceable, but it showed potential. A major attraction was a lot size of about half an acre, sloping downward to a brook at the rear edge of the property, some three hundred feet from the street.

The interior layout was jarring to me. The front door led right into the living room. There was no vestibule. A wide doorway, at one time enclosed by French doors, opened onto a large central room with a ceiling upon which faux beams had been installed. At the far end we spotted a timeworn kitchen with a drab linoleum floor covering.

To the left of the central room, a wooden door with inlaid, diamond-patterned glass in a Victorian style opened to a small hallway that led to two bedrooms. To the right a bathroom featured pink tile and porcelain fixtures.

Rising from the small hallway, a staircase provided access to the upper level, whose purpose seemed unclear. It was essentially attic space, as yet amorphous save for a blue-tiled bathroom with a window facing the backyard.

Comparing it to other homes on the market, we quickly realized that we were in no position to bid on any of them. My parents stepped up to kick in a generous amount for a down payment, but even with their help, the monthly mortgage expense was at the top of our limit.

We held fast in our subsequent negotiations, realizing that the woman seller, a divorcee with five children, was eager to close the deal on our final offer of thirty-six thousand dollars.

MY FIRST RUDE AWAKENING to what awaited us literally came on the day we moved in. Drained of energy and filthy after unloading the U-Haul truck we had rented, I went into the pink bathroom to take a shower but discovered that the handle of the valve to divert water into the showerhead was missing. I grabbed the pliers out of my toolbox and used it instead. Clean and refreshed, I brought the toolbox to the basement—when I spotted a puddle of water on the floor, right under the pink bathroom.

I soon realized that Mrs. Collins, having realized that the pipe feeding water to the showerhead was broken, simply removed the diverter handle, solving the problem by hiding it. Over time, I encountered other maintenance shortcomings, in general a reflection of how she had dealt with her life's circumstances by ignoring the root cause of her problems.

The pink bathroom shower problem was first on the list of home improvement projects I eventually undertook. As a novice homeowner, I came to rely heavily on Karen's father to become my mentor in the art of do-it-yourself home improvement. Weekly visits by Paul and Jean became routine.

We started by replacing the leaky old wood-framed windows with new, insulated sliding-vinyl ones. Next came the whole-house fan to improve the air circulation. For that task I came to rely on Brent, who had married Karen's former roommate, Irene. Brent had previously worked as a roofer and his expertise was invaluable.

To complete the climate control in the attic, Paul recommended we cut an opening through the street-facing exterior wall to push through an conditioner into a metal sleeve affixed to the wall. Between some friends to do the heavy lifting, and Paul's expert guidance and help with the electrical connection, we completed the task over a weekend.

WHEN KAREN BECAME A FULL-TIME MOM, our household income had dropped precipitously. With the new housing expense, our financial situation caused us to tighten our belts in order to put aside funds for capital improvements.

Serendipity landed one day while I was on the 167 Express bus on my commute to New York.

"Sam?" a familiar voice asked.

"Oh, my God, Roni! What are you doing here?"

I had first met Roni at City College but we had lost touch over the years.

"We moved to Teaneck and are renting an upstairs apartment in a two-family house," she said, settling into the vacant seat adjacent to mine. The unplanned reunion allowed us to spend the rest of the ride updating our lives, including our recent move to Teaneck with our toddler. "We need to get together," I said when we parted ways at the Port Authority Bus Terminal.

Our first encounter with Roni and her husband some weeks later was another of those inevitable moments of coincidence such as had occurred with the Meissner family, my in-laws' friends. Larry seemed familiar to me the minute the couple came in.

"I think I know you," I asked. "Where did you go to high school?"

"DeWitt Clinton."

"Of course! You were in Squad A, too!" I exclaimed, recalling that, while he was in my homeroom, he'd had no acting role in any of our stage productions, and consequently we had barely interacted at school.

Over time, we saw them frequently, and Roni, a social worker, developed a keen bond with our two-year-old daughter, who was highly conversant beyond her age. They were fond of Teaneck and decided to buy a home in town.

"I just hope it won't take too long for the closing," Roni said one day. "We just don't like living above the landlord," she added, hinting that they might need to rent elsewhere until they took title on the property.

Karen and I looked at one another, instinctively seeing a potential easing of our financial bind.

"Why don't you guys move upstairs while you're waiting," I proposed. "You'd have your own bedroom and bath upstairs, and we could set up a little commune and share meals."

They accepted our proposal and we agreed on a monthly rent that would go toward paying our mortgage.

Communal living worked out well for all of us over a period of several months. Roni's super culinary skills kept us well fed—let alone the benefit of the rental income we earned. Having them join our household formed a bond that has lasted a lifetime.

BY THE MID 1970S, MY FATHER HAD FOUND the proverbial American street that was paved with gold. As he expected, through a combination of hard work, imagination and ambition, America did make it possible for an immigrant to achieve a level of financial security and comfort to suit his desire for happiness.

Speedycut was not the biggest fish in the metalworking supply pond, but it won a respectable status in a smaller niche of vendors able to assemble efficient and reliable production centers that were somewhat automated with the emerging technology called numerical control.

In this pre-computerized stage of evolution to robotics, Speedycut not only supplied stand-alone metalworking machinery, but unlike many of its competitors, it fashioned the tapping machines, drill presses, lathes, and other task-specific components into labor- and time-saving custom machining centers. Under John Gronner's vision, this turned out to be a key competitive advantage, and his protégé Jeff Lafer successfully leveraged this capability to expand sales and increase margins.

After Roni and Larry moved to their new home a few blocks away, my father suggested that I apply my skills to supplement my ADL salary with some freelance work for Speedycut. To expand understanding of the company's core competencies and competitive advantage, he and Jeff asked me to develop some product brochures.

I discussed it with Karen, and we both agreed we could use the extra money. Though I loved my parents, I was initially hesitant to work for my father. He had been disappointed by my decision against becoming his apprentice to eventually inherit the business. But during our meetings, he came to appreciate my skills as a communications consultant, able to promote his business and drive sales. At these sessions, I was subjected to interminable lectures on metalworking concepts and intricate details of the inner workings of the machinery, yet he was impressed by how I was able to digest it all into crisp and straightforward marketing communications.

In all, I produced three brochures to highlight the versatile product line and even got into developing a print ad that sought to differentiate the company's unique design for a tapping machine component called a spindle head.

The Look-Alikes Don't Have Our Head For Tapping was the headline I conjured up, in a *Mad Men* kind of inspirational moment. The irony of all this did not escape me. I was now having a baptism by fire in the art of advertising, the career I had initially pursued but rejected because I had lacked the maturity and patience to fully understand its context, nuance and complexity.

Having founded a successful enterprise, my father now began to reap the benefits of the American tax system that was skewed in favor of moxie and entrepreneurship. Through those years, my parents went on whirlwind tours that were partially offset by tax-deductible Speedycut business expenses.

Aba became obsessed with collecting receipts he would submit to his accountant to prove legitimate business-related expenses he incurred in pursuit of sourcing and sales opportunities in India and China. While visiting Israel, my parents used the occasion to visit Sandler clan members, my mother's Eilat family branch, and the Holon *Jeckes* who remained in the country.

The visits to Europe always included a reunion with Rudy, Lydie, Jean-Luc, and Onkel Sylvain. I have no doubt that on these visits my father and uncle discussed and strategized the status of their claim for restitution from the East German authorities.

Restitution was the last thing on my mind. My father was no doubt gratified to see his American dream play out this way. His first-born son, now a father himself, had entered the middle class with a house on a half-acre plot of American soil.

As a thirty-something, with new family responsibilities, my daily focus of attention and energy veered to what were the primary needs of my wife and daughter: shelter, food, health and comfort. Although we spoke by phone often, and saw them while they were in New Jersey, my parents became peripheral to our daily routine.

Meanwhile my sister, having graduated from Northeastern University, remained in the Boston area, where she landed a teaching position at a private special needs school. She developed a close circle of friends through which she came to meet Wayne Kallman, a native of suburban Peabody.

For their wedding on November 13, 1977, Tammy and Wayne chose the same venue and rabbi that Karen and I had selected for our nuptials.

For Aba, grafting the Kallman branch to the same tree trunk onto which Karen's Widder clan was joined four years earlier marked the culmination of success he could never imagine. I pictured him as a young soldier, isolated in pre-State Israel, having learned not only that he had become an orphan in the Holocaust, but that his grandfather, so many uncles, aunts and cousins had perished. My eyes welled over in tears at my sister's wedding, surrounded by a reconstituted family, to see my father so happy, knowing as well that Karen was carrying his second grandchild.

But within three months of Tammy and Wayne's wedding Aba's euphoria came crashing down. Jean-Luc called with news that Rudy had died. My father immediately booked a flight to France to be at Lydie's side for the funeral. The non-denominational burial took place in the small cemetery of Plachy, site of the vacation home Rudy and Lydie had long hoped to become their retirement residence. Regrettably, he only managed to live there in retirement for several months.

My parents sold the original house from where Speedycut was launched and moved to a split-level on a cul-de-sac in Oradell, New Jersey. I was often called upon to check on the house and water the plants whenever Aba and Ima were in Florida during the winter. In time, these visits were extended, as more and more of their *Jecke* friends permanently relocated to the Sunshine State. Most importantly to my mother, by this time her sisters—Esther, now a widow, and Mady and Kuba—had bought apartments at Wynmoor, a major complex for the over-fifty-five crowd just off Interstate Route 95 in Coconut Creek, Florida.

CHAPTER 17

Redirection

I T'S TIME," KAREN SAID, WAKING ME on the early morning hours of Sunday July 16, 1978. We had pre-arranged the logistics for the trip to Roosevelt Hospital when Karen was entering labor. As planned, we brought Arielle to our neighbors Roni and Larry, and I sped across the George Washington Bridge and down the West Side Highway, reaching the hospital in seventeen minutes flat.

The baby boy would not wait. Dr. Mootabar rushed in and put on a surgical mask to cover the crumbs from his unfinished breakfast. "What's the rush?"

One push and all eight pounds and nine ounces of a screaming baby boy arrived promptly at eight-thirty.

I convinced Karen that we should have a traditional circumcision at home, although she preferred it be done in the hospital. To assuage her, we found a *mohel* with a medical degree. We chose the Hebrew name Shimshon for Jesse in memory of my mother's brother, who had died in 1974.

The main event took place in the big center room of the house. Though the bedrooms had air conditioning window units, the attic fan I had installed did little to ease the discomfort from the oppressive heat that day. Many of the women, notably my wife, escaped to the porch to avoid the actual procedure, but both grandfathers were active participants in the brief ceremony. One surprise guest attended as well. My childhood friend from Holon Roni Benjamin, had called me from New York a few days earlier. "Great to hear from you! You're just in time for my son's *brit milah*," I told him, using the modern Hebrew for circumcision. I had not seen him in decades, and here he was on the cusp of creating the next generation to follow our own.

THE ARRIVAL OF ANOTHER MOUTH TO FEED provided the impetus for again rethinking my career path. I was past thirty, having spent the past decade—one third of my life—in the same job at ADL. I feared my career options were closing, concerned that I would be typecast as a member of "the Jewish civil service" as many of my professional peers had proudly referred to themselves. I admired their dedication but soured on the idea of spending the rest of my life working for ADL or any of the other important Jewish-sponsored non-profits in its class.

I found the job of writer and editor at the national headquarters of the foremost human relations and Jewish defense agencies personally satisfying and meaningful. Yet I was beginning to feel hemmed in, knowing that my immediate boss was not ready to move on, limiting my upward mobility. I had remained through the succession of two of the agency's professional leaders, beginning with the appointment of Nathan Perlmutter to replace the longtime national director, Benjamin Epstein, and, upon his untimely death, with the ascension of Abraham Foxman to the post.

Redirection

My work was always interesting and challenging, and I had a chance to work with inspiring professionals who devoted their lives to strengthening democracy while fighting anti-Semitism. As part of ADL missions and meetings I had occasion to visit Israel and be exposed to top-level briefings at military installations, the Knesset, and the offices of Prime Minister Menachem Begin.

Still, as a paid staff member I was always conscious of the distinction between the professionals and the influential lay leaders who guided the agency, many of whom were financially successful people in the professions, business, and industry. I came to realize that it was quite honorable to be financially successful in commercial, for-profit endeavors and remain dedicated and active in a volunteer capacity on behalf of causes I deemed important.

I knew I had no interest in working for companies that promoted odious products like tobacco, but I was open to almost anything else. I began perusing the classified advertising section of the *New York Times,* and one day spotted an opening in the PR department of AT&T. All I knew about the brand at the time was that it was the long distance telephone company with the tagline, *Reach Out and Touch Someone.*

What animated me most in the classified ad was the name of Bruce Brackett, to whom I was supposed to address my resumé. Bruce was a journalist I had met years earlier at the *Bergen Record,* but he had subsequently left to work for Western Electric, the manufacturing arm of the Bell System.

I was able to reach him by phone and we caught up on each other's lives, both professional and personal.

"If you read the news, you should know that the Bell System is breaking up, and Western Electric is being restructured into the new AT&T," Bruce told me. "This job calls for a very strong writer to work in employee communication. It is an important role to help employees transition from a regulated monopoly into a competitive telecom business."

He told me the hiring manager had assigned him the task of screening resumés for consideration. "Do me a favor," he added, "knowing you and what you can do, better send your resumé to my house because I expect hundreds of responses. I'll make sure you get considered."

Some weeks passed before I was called for an interview at 222 Broadway, which had served as the Western Electric headquarters. There I had the strangest job interview in my career, run by a red-headed and bearded Mike Cocca, who was in charge of the internal communications functions for what had just become an entity called AT&T Technologies.

"The job is moving to New Jersey," he announced. "Do you have a problem with that?"

"Nope. I live in New Jersey. That's not a problem."

"Well, it is for me and my wife. We live in Brooklyn and love it, so we are not sure if we want to make that commute. Nor are we sure we want to move to the suburbs."

During the entire interview, Mike asked me very little about my experience and my skills. Mostly, he told me about his career, how he had come up through the ranks as a writer and editor of company publications, and how reluctant he was to move.

He then brought me to an unoccupied office next to his, sat me at an old-fashioned manual typewriter and told me I was required to take a writing test. "Here is a sample speech written for one of our executives. Just turn that into a press release."

Having worked on daily newspapers and a wire service, it took me a very short time to write a news story on the basis of the prepared remarks. I had time to look around a bit, noticed that the office belonged to someone named B.E. Nathan.

Several more weeks passed. One morning, when I was in my ADL office, the phone rang.

"Sam?" an assertive masculine voice on the end blurted out.

"Yes."

"This is Emmett Nathan. From Western...er...I mean AT&T. That's a terrific background you have for the job. Are you still interested?"

"Why, yes, of course," I said tentatively, wondering whether I had met him during my visit, until it dawned on me that I had met his office.

"You know what I liked best about your background? The *Newark News*. I was city editor there, and anyone who worked there in my book is automatically the kind of writer I want on my team."

I never imagined the series of coincidences—the mutual connection to the *Bergen Record* and my brief residency at the *Newark News*—would throw open the door of opportunity into a new corporate public relations career in technology. It could not have come at a better time to redirect my professional aspirations to my growing family responsibilities.

The redirection catapulted me into a new world that was completely unfamiliar to me. I was well versed in the mechanics of my craft, but I had to learn the art of socialization into a structured corporate hierarchy. I adapted quickly, even as many of my new colleagues were not as pliable in the fast-changing culture of the post-Divestiture AT&T.

AT&T Technologies moved to new quarters in Berkeley Heights, New Jersey, and I started spending a good time of my day commuting by car.

During prior summers, when ADL allowed me to take a full month off, we were able to replace the pink-tiled bathroom on the ground floor of our house and gut the kitchen. But now Karen and I discussed selling the house so that I would have a shorter commute and more time to spend with the family.

Our initial trip was to Clinton, New Jersey, where new homes were within our price range. But we found the suburban sprawl and cookie-cutter developments not to our taste. While it was a short drive to Berkeley Heights, it would not be practical for Karen, whose mobility was limited since she didn't have a driver's license.

We next explored another community near my office. Millburn reminded us of Teaneck—an older, established community with a well-defined downtown shopping area that invited pedestrian traffic. Through a local real estate broker we found and put down a deposit on an older home that displayed a lot of character both inside and out. But within a few weeks the agent called to let us know the owner had had a change of heart and was taking the house off the market.

Although disappointed, I continued my long daily commute and left the house-hunting to Karen, who preferred staying in Teaneck, where she had befriended other mothers with young children like ours. Her wish was realized in summer, 1986 when she found a newly refurbished center hall colonial several blocks away from our house. We promptly bought it when our first home sold within two days in a bidding contest between two prospects.

In the fall of the prior year, Tammy and Wayne, by then living in Redondo Beach, California, had learned that she was pregnant. The following March 28, twin boys were delivered by Cesarean section. Matthew Elliot was named for Karen's brother Erik Widder, who had lost his valiant fight against cancer on August 12, 1979; Benjamin's middle name—Rory—memorialized Onkel Rudy.

I came to sense that once he reached age sixty-six several weeks later, my father had begun to see himself as the titular head of his own revitalized Gronner clan; the loss of kin he had suffered was beginning to be refilled with his own two children, their spouses, and four of their offspring. As he took stock of his life experiences, he assumed the role of patriarch, with the responsibility of advising some his fatherless nieces, his brother's son, and preserving his generation's legacy for his descendants.

We had enrolled Arielle in the religious school of a small Reform congregation in Teaneck in preparation for her bat mitzvah, which we marked at the synagogue in spring, 1987, followed by a catered reception at our new home.

My father was never one to attend synagogue services, even though my mother had joined the sisterhood of the Conservative synagogue in Bergenfield. I do not recall either of them attending regular worship there.

But perhaps in deference to our affiliation, my father agreed to be a guest speaker at our congregation to mark the fiftieth anniversary of *Kristallnacht*. He asked me to help shape his words to tell his personal story for maximum impact on a contemporary generation of American Jews—especially youngsters.

He focused on his own childhood experience:

> *An event like Kristallnacht could not happen without a consistent, unending hate campaign. I had seen this happen years earlier when I was only ten years old. The same age as my grandson Jesse is now.*
>
> *I lived in small town that is now in East Germany. There were only a few Jewish families. So naturally, most of my school chums were Christian.*
>
> *...It's true that those from working-class families did not socialize with us, both Jewish and Christian, who had been accepted to the special middle school. So, much like today, we were friendlier with each other than with the kids from*

other schools.

My classmates and I tended to go to each other's birthday parties, and even weddings of older brothers and sisters. Except for Christmas. That was when my parents drew the line. And that was the only time I felt different.

In September 1930 the Nazi Party staged a march through the town. They wore mustard-colored uniforms, black boots and red swastika armbands. This was election time in the province where I lived. The Nazis shouted awful slogans: "Juda Verrecke, Deutschland erwecke." Loosely Translated: "Awake, Germany and rid yourself of the rotten Jews."

Being only ten, I couldn't fully understand why these people would say such terrible things. But the next day I personally felt the effect of such talk. One of my buddies refused to walk to school with us. During recess, he saw me approach and quickly joined a group with whom none of us was friendly. He pretended not to know me. A few days later, when we were alone, I confronted him. I asked why he disliked me so suddenly. He said he no longer wanted contacts with Jews. "They are a blister on the body of the German people," he said, repeating what he heard at home.

This was the first time I had heard my father publicly talk about his personal childhood experience with hateful words. He went on to describe his family story, but this being a public setting, he saw it as a chance to drive home a lesson that would motivate me years later to perpetuate it, as I am doing here.

Kristallnacht was not an embarkation point for the Holocaust. It was only an interim stop along a calculated route of destruction. It began years earlier when some goose-stepping hoodlums marched through my little town of Ilmenau.

This is something to keep in mind. The next time you hear someone mak-

ing disparaging remarks about a group of people, don't sit back. Speak out. Organize. Stay informed, and let others know about this constant danger. Even today it is with us. Witness the appearance of David Duke on the ballot in yesterday's election. A repackaged grand dragon of the Ku Klux Klan was running for President. Right here, in Bergen County.

It can't happen here? That's what my parents thought, too.

CHAPTER 18

Restitution and Reclamation

"General Secretary Gorbachev, if you seek peace, if you seek prosperity for the Soviet Union and Eastern Europe, if you seek liberalization, come here to this gate. Mr. Gorbachev, open this gate. Mr. Gorbachev, tear down this wall!"

O N JUNE 12, 1987, PRESIDENT RONALD REAGAN issued this challenge as he stood behind bulletproof glass on a specially erected platform in front of the Brandenburg Gate, an iconic symbol that had marked the dividing line between the democratic West Berlin and the repressive eastern side.

It would take another two years for the Soviet empire to collapse, but as he watched the disintegration unfold, my father, an astute student of history, was preparing for the likely fall of the repressive East German regime. It would mean that his longstanding claim for restitution of the family's inheritance would at last be addressed.

With Rudy's passing, Aba was by default the primary claimant for restitution. He had begun to lay the groundwork by obtaining the necessary power-of-attorney documents to act on behalf of Lydie and Jean-

Luc as inheritors of his brother's rights for compensation.

Though keenly aware of the geopolitical changes in the Soviet sphere, I paid scant attention to my father's personal chess game strategy as he monitored the developments, especially the events in East Germany. I was forty then and focused on my own career path within the new AT&T company, which was still in the throes of reconfiguring its corporate structure to best adapt to the deregulated telecommunications landscape.

We were again at the cusp of yet another rearrangement of the European political boundaries, just as had occurred throughout the millennia. The military might that had forcefully held together the Union of Soviet Socialist Republics was disentangling before my father's eyes, and East Germany was one of the first to realize the futility of holding its population behind walls and barbed wire.

It happened in rather dramatic fashion when the longtime East German Communist Party strongman Erich Honecker was ousted on October 18, 1989. A succession of futile attempts to introduce reforms while maintaining the embedded Communist Party infrastructure led the East German populace to rise up in protest two weeks later.

On November fourth, a Saturday, thousands turned out for street demonstrations in Dresden, Magdeburg, Schwerin and Berlin, calling for free elections. The following Tuesday, the entire cabinet resigned and half of the governing Politburo members were ousted and were immediately replaced.

As recalled by the former Eastern Europe bureau chief for *Newsweek,* "The dramatic fall of the infamous Berlin Wall, the symbol of five decades of Cold War, played out almost as farce." Following the hasty reorganization of the government, the role of party spokesman had been assigned to a longtime party functionary, Günter Schabowski.

[He] dropped in on his boss en route to his daily press conference, itself an innovation for the secretive, all-controlling Communists.

"Anything to announce?" he asked casually. The party chief, Egon Krenz, thought for a moment, then handed Mr. Schabowski a two-page memo. "Take this," he said with a grin. "It will do us a power of good."

Mr. Schabowski scanned it in his limo. It seemed straightforward: a brief on legislation his boss forced through a reluctant Parliament that very afternoon that would give East Germans the right to travel to the West—and in doing so make the new regime the heroes of the people. At the press conference, he read it out as item four or five on a list of sundry announcements. It had to do with passports. Every East German would now, for the first time, have a right to one. They could go where they wanted, including to the West.

For a people locked for so long behind the Iron Curtain, this was momentous news. There was a sudden hush, then a ripple of excited murmuring. Mr. Schabowski droned on. From the back of the room, as the cameras rolled, broadcasting live to the nation, a reporter shouted out the fateful question. "When does it take effect?"

Mr. Schabowski paused, looked up, suddenly confused. "What?"

The chorus of questions rang out again. Mr. Schabowski scratched his head, mumbled to aides on either side, perched his glasses on the end of his nose, shuffled through his papers, looked up—and shrugged. "Ab sofort." Immediately. Without delay.

With that, the room (and the world) erupted. We now know that Mr. Schabowski was largely oblivious to the earthquake his words had caused. In fact, he had returned from a short vacation that very day. He didn't know that the new rules were supposed to take effect the next day, Nov. 10—subject to all sorts of fine print, including the requirement to obtain visas. East Germans didn't, either. All they knew was what they had just heard on radio and TV. Thanks to Mr. Schabowski, they thought they were free to go. Now. Ab sofort.

Restitution and Reclamation

> By the tens of thousands, in a human tide not unlike that descending on
> Europe today, they converged on Checkpoint Charlie and other crossing points
> to West Berlin. Surprised and overwhelmed, receiving no instructions and not
> knowing what else to do, East German border police acted on their own. Like
> Mr. Schabowski, they shrugged—and threw open the gates to freedom. And so
> the Berlin Wall came down.[28]

The date of November 9, 1989, when East Germans shed the yoke
that had locked them inside their own country, will forever coincide with
the anniversary of *Pogromnacht,* the officially sanctioned Nazi campaign
against Germany's Jews exactly fifty-one years earlier. Henceforth the
two historic events will inexorably be bound into a single indelible lesson
about humanity's bipolar proclivities—on one hand, a penchant for utter
cruelty—and on the other, an irrepressible yearning for liberty.

THE UPHEAVAL IN THE WAKE of the Soviet Union's demise illustrated
how a number of well-connected individuals were able to parlay the
chaos to their advantage, resulting in what we now recognize as a pow-
erful cadre of oligarchs who maneuvered their way to the top of Russia's
political and economic elite.

On a much smaller scale—and with none of the oligarchs' sinister
motives—my father theorized that a period of uncertainty about private
property rights in a post-Communist East Germany offered a window
of opportunity to revive his longstanding claim for restitution. Moreover,
the disastrous economic state of former East German states like Thüringen left the public coffers depleted of cash; hence, he reasoned, the
bureaucrats minding the *Amt für Vermögensfragen* (in charge of the trust
of Jewish property and postwar nationalized assets) would soon be over-
whelmed with restitution claims.

Within months of the formal reunification on October 3, 1990, my parents booked a flight to Germany, and my father returned to his native Ilmenau for the first time in fifty-four years. The *Bauhaus*-style building his parents had built still stood at its location. The showroom was locked, but he was able to peer through its ample vitreous windows and peruse the interior of the now-shuttered furniture and carpeting retail store, as were most local operations of the *Handelsorganization (HO)*—the East German nationalized trade group.

Prior to making the journey, Aba had been in contact with Heinz Geitz, a locally connected attorney whom he considered able to smooth the longstanding claim through the entrenched bureaucracy.

Indeed, by the time of my father's arrival, Herr Geitz had arranged a meeting with the officials who managed all the assets held in trust, including those of former Jewish owners.

This is when Aba first learned that there was another claimant for same property: The Näder family, whose store had been seized and nationalized after war, had also sought restitution for what they deemed an injustice by the communist authorities.

Mr. Geitz presented the litany of evidence my father had provided.

"Mr. Gronner, what is it you are looking for in ways of compensation?" one of the bureaucrats asked.

"I am not asking for financial damages," my father noted, well aware that neither the state of Thüringen nor the city of Ilmenau were in a position to pay out a cash settlement. "I merely ask that the property stolen from my parents be returned to my family as our legacy."

The exchange had an impact on everyone, including Hartmut Näder, who thereafter relinquished his family's claim. So impressed was he that he wrote a subsequent letter to my father in which he enclosed his father's postwar financial statements, which he had planned to submit as evidence to support his family's claim, along with photographs of the store's interiors:

> *July 30, 1991*
> Dear Mr. Gronner:
> We, my sister and I, would like to thank you very much for our conversation last weekend.
> We got to know a very tolerant, open-minded person who always had to gain positive sides in the struggle for life.
> Your words will resonate in us.
> As mentioned, I will send you the necessary documents about the construction of the house as well as some other documents that might be of use to you.

Prior to my parents' return home, my father had assigned Herr Geitz to settle the details of the transfer of title to himself and his brother's estate.

My father regaled us with the sequence of events and the success of his mission. The Gronner family would once again resume ownership of the land and building my grandparents had erected in Ilmenau to house the Wilhelm Sandler store, including the upstairs residence where my father had lived from age nine until his departure for Palestine at age sixteen.

But what was to become of it?

It's a question my father discussed with me, my sister, Jean-Luc, and Lydie. The verdict was unanimous: Yes, we all valued the symbolism of reclaiming this legacy, but no one had an interest in living in Ilmenau nor of becoming landlords should it become valuable rental property. Once it was back in the family's hands, we'd see if it was salvageable, and if so, sell it and split the proceeds as our family legacy.

It took several months for Herr Geitz to complete all the paperwork to clear the property for sale. That is how I came to accompany my parents on the May 1992 trip to Ilmenau—the one that impressed me so much in the stark difference between the vibrant West Germany and its estranged sibling, the eastern side, a postwar pawn in four decades of Cold War.

My father had booked us at the Gabelbach, a resort that had served the upper crust of the East German regime—people deemed worthy of some sort of reward or benefit by virtue of their status within the party apparatus.

By East German standards, the accommodations were luxurious, but a keen observer could easily discern the neglect and lack of maintenance in the worn floor coverings and cracked walkways that connected the various outbuildings. The place featured an indoor pool, but I could not fathom the purpose of the rusted stationary bicycle on the pool deck. Was it intended to showcase the imagined upscale amenities, or (as I concluded,) was it a relic that was just there because, in the forty years of top-down hierarchical control, no one had dared ask that it be removed or replaced?

In any case, the accommodations were adequate for the mission of the trip, and the ample breakfast buffet selection of *Wurst, Speck,* and *Rollmops* satiated our appetite for a good part of the day.

We left my mother at the hotel when my father and I made our way to the family heirloom. In another instant of amorphous boundaries, the street address, No. 3 Moltkestrasse, had by then been reassigned to a new postal destination, No. 7 Friedrich-Hoffmann Strasse. The main commercial district of the oldest part of Ilmenau was being converted into a pedestrian mall, so there was no vehicular traffic, rendering the neighborhood relatively quiet except for footsteps reverberating from the buildings on either side, interspersed with clipped conversations from passersby.

While he had been outside the building during his prior visit, my father used the key supplied by Herr Geitz to hesitantly open the door and step into the ground-level sales floor for the first time in fifty-six years. Herr Geitz had made sure that all the contents were cleaned out prior to our arrival.

There was a slight musty odor in the air, a sign of water penetration, but the wood finish on the walls all appeared intact. Craning his neck up toward the second level forced his jaw to drop and mouth to open. Exhaling, he could only muster a short whispered utterance: "Wow!"

I could tell how his memory called him back, as if the Wilhelm Sandler store was still teeming with shoppers and salespersons, with racks of suits, trousers, coats, and jackets arrayed in separate areas. Toward the rear, the wooden staircase rose to a landing and veered to the left, its distinctive *Bauhaus* style preserved as if time had stood still.

The residence was accessible by way of a side entrance around the corner, an alley by then renamed Spitalgasse. In trepidation, we ascended the stairwell that led into the expansive apartment. The kitchen was brightly lit by the window facing the alley. "Whenever my friends rang the bell I looked out this window and saw who it was," Aba told me. "If I was in the right mood, I'd take a glass with some water and pour it on their heads just for laughs," he chuckled.

As he explored the dark wooden kitchen cabinets, he murmured, "Nothing has changed. Everything is the way I remember."

I walked out of the kitchen into what had been the main family room in the middle of the apartment, over which rows of fluorescent lights imparted an air of office space. In fact, the residence had been used for many years as the offices of the trust that managed all the formerly private assets that had either been "aryanized" by the Nazi regime or nationalized after the war by the Communist authorities. In the case of this very building, dispossession had occurred in both instances.

"I don't believe it!" I heard my father gasp from the kitchen and I immediately ran back in and found that his eyes welled over.

"What is it?"

He opened a cabinet door. "Do you see these three holes?" he pointed out.

"Yes. What was that?" I asked.

"These are screw holes. This is where the coffee mill was attached," he explained. "It was my job to grind coffee every morning for my mother," His voice broke, and he began to sob.

We made our way up to the attic level, the former living quarters of the caretaker, where we found the source of the mildew—there were signs of water penetration through the flat roof, indicating that a major repair needed to be undertaken. To my father, that meant that the prospective buyers Herr Geitz had secured had to have a substantial amount of cash.

For this reason, when we met him after the inspection, Aba and I both agreed that the former manager of the nationalized furniture business would not have the resources to secure the necessary financing. The other bidder was an established chain of stores based in what had been West Germany, eager to plant a seed in soil that had lain fallow as the East German economy floundered. The New Yorker chain was eager to close the deal, and my father agreed.

Herr Geitz immediately got on the phone and called his counterpart in Braunschweig. "They will send their helicopter tomorrow and you can close the deal," he told my father after hanging up.

Neither my father nor I slept well that night. He was ruminating about the decision to part with his childhood home.

My restlessness, though related, veered in another direction. Lacking the personal attachment Aba had felt to the bricks and mortar, and the sweat equity his parents had invested, my notion of legacy took a practical turn—the financial security he had sought for his family by leaving Israel. Yet that night I was inspired to propose something to relieve him of the personal anguish.

Over breakfast, before leaving for the Erfurt airport, I said: "Aba, I have an idea for a clause to add to the sales contract. There are no grave markers for your parents—what if we obligate the buyer to install a memorial plaque to them, so that the people of Ilmenau know that this property was once an establishment owned by Samuel and Helene Gronner, who were victims of the Shoah?"

"That's a wonderful idea," he said. "I will bring this up so we can add it to the contract."

MY FATHER SAT IN FRONT WITH THE PILOT, and I strapped myself into the bench in the rear. I had previously flown in a helicopter at my basic training for the National Guard. But over the roar of the engine, I could not hold a conversation, so I sat silently during the half-hour flight to Braunschweig.

Surprisingly, the chauffeur-driven car dispatched to us whisked us, not to the New Yorker corporate offices, but rather the offices of the company's law firm. Gundolf Tessmann, personal attorney and representative of Friedrich Knapp, CEO of New Yorker, greeted us warmly.

After some pleasantries, he handed my father a copy of the contract he had drawn up in prior consultation with Herr Geitz, representing my father and the estate of Rudolphe Gronner.

As was his manner over many years of contract negotiations on behalf of Speedycut, Aba took his time perusing the seven-page document. Characteristically, despite numerous prior reviews by Herr Geitz, he did find a couple of nits and both he and Herr Tessmann initialed the agreed changes.

With the contract formalities concluded, Aba then addressed the attorney. "My son made a very good observation, and I would like to incorporate an addendum to the contract in which the purchaser of my family home and business agree to the installation of a marker commemorating the history of the property. As you know, there are no grave markers for my parents, and would you agree on behalf of the buyer to permit me to place such a memorial on the building?"

"Absolutely," the lawyer answered without hesitation. And it became a done deal.

CHAPTER 19

Life Fulfilled

I N THE SUMMER OF 1993, my parents visited Ilmenau again for the dedication of the memorial plaque above the tall storefront windows of the former department store. This time, my sister and her husband Wayne accompanied them. The ceremony became an official public event that drew media coverage.

An Ilmenauer Cares for the Remembrance of His Parents read the headline of the July 13, 1993, edition of the daily *Ilmenauer Allgemeine* newspaper. Displayed on the front page of the local section under photos of the event, the caption highlighting the images read, *Remembrance of the fate of the Gronner family from Ilmenau.*

It was only the first manifestation of remembrance of the Gronner family in the very place that the Nazi-led government had sought to eradicate my surname.

In 2002, the Gronner family was named in the first public Holocaust memorial erected by the municipality in Wetzlarer Platz, the main square of the old city. My grandparents' names are among the thirty on the city's memorial to former Jewish neighbors deported and murdered during the Nazi regime.

Although he had been invited, my father was unable to attend and instead asked an American acquaintance he had met in Ilmenau to deliver his remarks. Matthew Cholomondeley, a businessman from Blue Ash, Ohio, was a frequent visitor to my father's hometown and a guiding force behind the Ilmenau-Blue Ash sister city relationship.

Years later, Matt told me that he had been criticized by his Blue Ash colleagues for reading my father's remarks in public, because the text named individuals whom Matt characterized as "fellow travelers or worse to the Nazi cause." Matt said that the then-mayor of Blue Ash "was horrified that I would read the names of these people! He said their grandchildren might be offended. I maintained I was the courier of John Gronner's words and would not alter it for political correctness."

The remarks were the beginning of my father's personal mission to testify as a witness to the events he had lived through in Ilmenau, and to urge the subsequent generations to be vigilant:

> It gives a special satisfaction and a sense of honor in this place (in full view of the department store of my parents) to be able to experience this event. I am—as no one else here—eyewitness of the development of German history, along with the development of the City of Ilmenau, from the days of the Weimar Republic (back to 1926) to the reunification of the divided Germany.
>
> Over this passage of years I lived through all sides of German culture, partly conveyed during the Goethe Memorial Week, through my teachers at the Goetheschule and at the former technical high school, but sadly also saw the shady side of this culture, exhibited through the character of Richard Walter, the local Nazi group leader and mayor; by Willy Marschler, the NS Prime Minister of the State of Thüringen; and by Messrs. Stabernach, Reimann, and

Schöps, who all earned their spurs during the Jew baiting in Ilmenau.

I look back with appreciation to the democratic, humane attitudes of student advisor Dr. Götze, the principal, Dr. Bayer, and lastly Professor Schmidt, who, despite enduring pressure from the Nazis, directed me toward the path of engineering that eventually saved my life.

Today I think of the members of the small Jewish congregation who on the occasion of the High Holy Days were able gather in the prayer room on Burggasse in order to practice the rituals of our faith. The assimilation of the Jewish community of this city was so complete that it was simply unimaginable that a nation that had brought forth Goethe, Schiller, Schopenhauer, Hegel, and Beethoven would be capable of transporting righteous fellow citizens to mass extermination camps in Poland. The German people had to make heavy sacrifices for this madness, but this was their free choice at the ballot box.

Two generations later, we are at this place to honor a new generation of German people who have learned a deep lesson from the criminals of the war generation and their fellow travelers.

Nations and people of all colors, races, or different beliefs must learn how to get along with one another in peace. It is not the sword that decides, but the knowledge that people react in different ways. This requires a conviction in mutual tolerance.

Fifty-six million victims of the Second World War demonstrate that a creative and accomplished society can achieve more important tasks than mutual annihilation. Disease, epidemic, and poverty are our challenges today. Advancing medical research is an attainable goal for mankind's current and future generations. This should be the guiding principle of this memorial, coupled with the pledge, Never Again.

By and large, my parents enjoyed their lifestyle as the twentieth century was closing. They purchased a house in Coconut Creek, down the road from the Wynmoor apartment complex where my mother's sisters lived. By this time, Karen's parents had sold their Brooklyn home of more than four decades and settled in Boca Raton, enabling occasional get-together among the in-laws.

PAUL AND JEAN WERE BY THEN in deteriorating health. The untimely loss of their son had taken a toll on them, and though both developed diabetes, Paul was also diagnosed with Parkinson's disease while Jean's heart condition worsened. Thankfully, my aunt Esther had connected them with an affable and generous Caribbean woman named Donna, whom they hired to help with the housework. She provided invaluable help to Jean, and their bond evolved into genuine friendship during Paul's frequent hospitalizations and extended rehabilitation.

By 1999, Karen and I made plans to relocate them to the campus of the Daughters of Miriam, a complex of residential facilities in Clifton, New Jersey, where Jean could live independently while Paul was cared for in the acute care home across the parking lot. But Paul died shortly before the move, and Jean moved there by herself, living in an apartment she came to love.

We frequently visited my mother-in-law, often bringing in some essentials she wanted picked up at the store. We would also take her to a New Jersey diner nearby. Among other tasks, she relied on me to change the Brita water filters in the jug she kept in the refrigerator.

Her heart blockage worsened, and she miraculously recovered from surgery none of us thought she would survive. But in March 2002 we were at her apartment when we witnessed the effects of a devastating stroke that landed her in the hospital again. This time she did not survive, and she died on April 3, 2002, at age 77.

Life Fulfilled

IN COMPARISON TO MY IN-LAWS, both younger than my parents, Aba and Ima were blessed to live through more joyous occasions. The year following Jean's death, our daughter Arielle was married to Brendan Gartland in an outdoor ceremony on the grounds of the Applegate Inn, a bed and breakfast resort that we had fully rented for the wedding party weekend.

My parents were also able to travel to Portland, Oregon, to attend the wedding of our son Jesse and Leah Fackeldey, who had resettled from Houston, Texas, to join the energy firm where they both worked.

At one point, my father gleefully informed me that he had purchased a place in New Jersey so they could spend their summers close to us, as well as to their friends from their days in Bergenfield who had relocated nearby. The Four Seasons complex was a planned adult community with the requisite tennis courts, but it was some eighty miles from our home—a drive in excess of an hour.

Given his age, Aba was still mentally acute, and loved his Mercedes C-Class 280, which he had driven down from New Jersey. Whether in New Jersey or Florida, he made a point of getting out on the tennis court and playing tournaments organized by the local tennis club.

As one would expect, many of my parents' aging *Jecke* friends developed infirmities; these were the usual topic of conversation when they gathered for their dinner parties and coffee klatches. Increasingly, these became daytime affairs, because many of those friends were reluctant to drive in the dark.

Meanwhile, as with most men his age, Aba had developed prostate cancer. He underwent laser treatment, and it seemed that whenever I called thereafter he was indisposed in the bathroom. He also came down with a bad case of shingles and gout, with pain and discomfort so intense that he mostly gave up his passion for playing tennis.

My mother was prone to frequent falls, both at home and outside. She had a history of such stumbles; I recall a specific family trip to New Hampshire as a teen, when she emerged from our motel room atop a steep hill. Not heeding our calls to take the longer but gentling sloping path, she lost her footing and rolled down head over heels as Aba captured the incident on his eight-millimeter camera.

Much later, living in Bergenfield, she had a serious driving accident that resulted in knee surgery. Some years thereafter, in my parents' second home in Oradell, she underwent rotator cuff surgery and, while still recuperating, her arm still in a sling, she tumbled down the basement stairs along with the basket of laundry she had foolishly decided to wash. She'd had limited mobility in her arm ever since.

Once in Florida, neither of my parents told us about my mother's falls, but these became evident when my sister and I visited and noticed her lingering bruises and the bandages my father fashioned. In addition to her physical challenges, her mental acuity and awareness were fading, and she was increasingly disoriented. Unable to easily get around, she tried to hang on to her network of family and friends each day, going down the list of names in her phone directory, just to say hello. In her confusion, she often repeated phone calls to the same person, not realizing she had already been in touch. She also called friends in Israel and Germany, forgetting the time differences, and woke them in the middle of the night.

The life of the snowbird was becoming too rigorous for my parents. They made only one more trip together, to sell their apartment in New Jersey and gather any remaining personal items they would ship to Florida.

But for my father there would be one more unexpected trip to the Northeast. Without my frail mother, whom he left behind in the care of aides, he flew to Boston in May 2009 upon learning that his son-in-law, Wayne, had collapsed at home from a massive subdural hematoma. Wayne had gone into a coma, from which we were told he could not recover. Tammy, her twin boys, and Wayne's siblings were locked up for hours behind doors, consulting with doctors at Brigham Women's Hospital in Boston until the immediate family reached the end-of-life decision.

The pall over all of us was unimaginable. Still, rising to the occasion, the Kallman family managed within a few days to pull together a gathering celebrating the memory of Wayne, who had died in the prime of life, short of reaching age fifty-six.

For Aba, it was surely a time of reckoning with his own mortality. He was a year from reaching his ninth decade and could barely reconcile the fact that his child's husband had predeceased him.

On the other side of the scale, Wayne's memorial was the last time my father would be in the presence of the assembled family. While his primary goal was to console his grieving daughter and her Kallman kin, the occasion served to share the loss with the succeeding Gronner generations. His progeny had by then expanded beyond four grandchildren to three great-grandchildren—Liora Gartland, Maia Gronner, and her three-week- old brother Jacob, who was alternatively snuggled in Leah's and Jesse's arms.

AT VARIOUS TIMES, WHILE THEY WERE STILL able to travel, Tammy and I had tried to coax our parents to plan for the eventuality that they would reach a point where Ima would require the help of aides—personal care that would free Aba from the burden. On one trip, Tammy had arranged for my father to look at senior housing facilities that would combine independent living for him with additional in-house staff to tend to Ima's personal care. He even agreed to put down a deposit on a well-appointed facility in a former textile mill in North Andover, a few minutes' drive from Tammy and Wayne's home in Salem, New Hampshire.

He ultimately decided against the idea. He fell back on the trope he had often cited for remaining in Florida, because it was what Ima wanted—to be close to her sisters. His stubbornness infuriated us, especially as we monitored their declining living situation in their late eighties.

The year after Wayne's passing signaled a steady decline as my father's role of caregiver for my mother drained him of energy. His patience grew short, burdened by an interminable repetition of mundane questions he had answered moments earlier. They fell into a tedious routine, orchestrating their excursions around doctor appointments and physical therapy sessions. While he had always liked tinkering around the house, he was now too exhausted, no longer motivated to maintain their Coconut Creek home. He put the house on the market, and my parents moved into the Wynmoor complex, where my aunts Mady and Esther lived.

When Tammy and I came down for a visit, we knew the arrangement could not last.

"Please come back north so we can be of help," we pleaded with Aba. "Ima needs more attention than you can give her. It's not as if you're really able to take advantage of the Florida climate," I pointed out.

"Your mother wants to be near her sisters," he answered.

It was a futile effort to get him to change his mind. And Tammy and I reluctantly came to rely on a stock phrase to reach the inevitable next phase: Events will drive decisions.

They ended up in the new place for only a brief stay, because my mother's mental state and physical deterioration required more attention and time than he was able to provide. In his mind, she needed to live in an assisted living facility that was better equipped to help her with her daily activities. This level of help, he reasoned, would free him to tend to their finances, which included juggling bank balances from various accounts to pay medical professionals, credit card bills, and buy groceries. He regularly received small checks from savings and investment accounts, as well as insurance reimbursements, and would then slowly climb into his Mercedes and drive to the bank to make a deposit. The routine kept him occupied, his mind active, and most of all, freed him from my mother's ceaseless questions—comforted by the knowledge she was being cared for by aides.

ON THE EVENING OF JULY 21, 2010, Karen and I were out with friends at a local Italian restaurant when my mobile phone rang.

"Yeah, Amnon, this is Esther," my aunt said though I recognized her voice. "So, your father fell and I gave him a pain pill and he is now comfortable."

"*What?*" I yelled into the phone. "What do you mean, you gave him a pain pill? Did a doctor look at him? What pill did you give him?"

"He had some here in the house. I gave him one, and he is now comfortable."

My blood curdled when I heard that my aunt, whose formal education had culminated in a beauty school certificate, had made a medical decision without consulting a professional.

She explained that she had been visiting my parents at the assisted living place they had moved into some months earlier. Someone from the staff had brought Aba in from the driveway, where he had fallen while climbing out of the car with the takeout package from the Pollo Loco chicken outlet. Great, I thought. The meal plan is included in his monthly fee, but he feels compelled to go out and bring home fast food.

"He'll be alright," my aunt tried to assure me.

"OK, thanks for being there," I replied, barely suppressing my anger and skepticism. My next call was to my sister, to let her know what had occurred, how pissed I was.

Early the next morning, our home phone rang.

"Amnon, you have to come down. I'm in awful pain."

"What do you mean?" I asked Aba. "I'm in *New Jersey*! Esther told me you fell. You need to call 9-1-1! I can't help you right now. You need to go to the *hospital*."

His voice was strained, barely a whisper. "All right, but you have to come down, please."

As I suspected, no amount of medication could alleviate the pain of a broken hip, the diagnosis I received later that day from the attending ER physician. It would require a hip replacement and long recovery.

The expected "event" that Tammy and I long anticipated had arrived. We were ready to implement the decision we had made to move Ima to a facility we had already seen and liked in Peabody, Massachusetts. The place was especially suited for Ima because it incorporated a self-contained impaired-memory unit, where the spacious single occupancy room with private bath opened to an expansive area designed as a town square.

It took us several days to secure her spot as we mentally prepared to visit Aba after he had undergone surgery. Mady and Esther kindly visited him and also saw to it that Ima had the care she needed.

Tammy and I coordinated our arrival in Fort Lauderdale and showed up at our father's bedside within days of his surgery. We assured him that Ima was well cared for, and that he ought to focus on getting better. His body language signaled an air of dejection, as if saying to himself, "How did it come to be that, at a time when she is most frail, so dependent, my wife can no longer rely on me as a source of guidance and support?"

Tammy and I held back the news of our decision to bring Ima north as long as possible. We feared his reaction, having been so adamant that they remain in Florida.

After the three weeks of Medicare-covered hospitalization, Aba was transferred on August 13 to a nearby rehabilitation facility. He was facing up to eight weeks of rigorous daily therapy sessions.

"Aba, we are going to make it easy for you to just concentrate on getting better and getting out of here," I told him as my sister's eyes welled up. "We are moving Ima to be near Tammy so you no longer have to worry about her."

There was no visible reaction. He sat there passively, languid and no longer insisting that she needed to be near her sisters. He had forced himself to acknowledge that, in her current state, she could no longer remember when she had last been with either Mady or Esther—even if it had been on the same day. She was wrapped in the fog of dementia, and it would no longer matter whether she was in Florida or Massachusetts.

"Now, it is entirely up to you," I cautioned him. "We are going to Boston with Ima, and then I will take a train home. We'd made plans to be with Jesse's family in Oregon, so I will be away for a week or so. It will give you time to get your physical therapy, regain your strength, and figure out what you will do next. You have choices. You can stay in Florida. Or you're welcome to join Ima up north. It is entirely up to you," I emphasized, knowing how he clung to his independence and free will.

"But, Aba, you'll need to eat and regain your strength," I added, referring to the complaints he had made to Mady about the hospital food he refused to eat. "If you don't eat, you will die," I declared bluntly. "And if that happens, *that* is *your* choice, and we will support your decision."

It was a cold-hearted thing to say. But I was sensing that he was seriously contemplating his own demise. That was the underlying reason for his call to me on the morning following his fall. It was not a request to drive him to the hospital; it was a call for final resolution of his affairs, a conscious decision to tie up any loose ends in his life, knowing full well that he had pretty much accomplished what he had set out to do. Doubtful of his ability to again get behind the steering wheel of his Mercedes, and afraid that clinging to unencumbered independence was now impossible, I sensed he was ready to do what he had always euphemistically called "close my eyes."

After our visit to Oregon, Karen and I boarded the flight to Newark on August 25; and as the crew was announcing that the doors had closed and it was necessary to turn off all electronics, my phone came alive with a call.

"Mr. Gronner," the voice at the other end announced, identifying himself as the attending physician at the rehab center. "I'm afraid your father is unresponsive."

"Oh, my God. . . Doctor, you've caught me on a plane and I've just been instructed to shut off the phone. Thank you for your call, but would you please call my sister and keep her updated? Do you have her number?"

"Yes, is it Tamar Kallman?"

"Yes, thank you. I will not be reachable for about six hours. Please confer with her in the interim."

Karen and I barely spoke for the duration. Both of us whimpered, as my mind raced, thinking that, by some miracle he would be revived by the time we landed. It was not to be.

Tammy had been extremely efficient during the hours we were in flight, deciding that we would bury Aba at a cemetery close to where Ima could visit. Moreover, she engaged a local funeral home familiar with Jewish ritual burials.

My father died with none of his relatives at his bedside. The only witness was Myrtle, an aide I tracked down some weeks later.

"Could you please tell me what happened?" I asked when I reached her by phone.

"Your father had returned from PT. He was exhausted, and sat down in the armchair," she recalled in a lilting Jamaican accent. "He asked me to please hand him a pillow, and I helped him get comfortable."

"And then what happened?"

"He said, 'Thank you very much,' and closed his eyes. Moments later he just slumped over."

Jochen Gronner died the way he had lived his life. Determined to control his own fate, to reclaim his inheritance, to rebuild a family and restore its reputation despite efforts to obliterate both, and to ensure that the legacy he left would sustain his widow, his children and their progeny.

A year later, it would inspire me to write the epitaph on the headstone at the Children of Israel Cemetery in Haverhill, Massachusetts: *A Life Fulfilled*.

TAMMY AND I HAD ALWAYS REGARDED OUR MOTHER as the weaker, frailer parent, yet she outlived our father by almost two years. Although her mobility declined along with her cognition, she seemed reinvigorated by Tammy's frequent visits bearing personal care products and clothes. Vera relished being taken to the designated children's play area at the facility for the aged. It was well stocked with toys for visiting young children like her great-grandchild Liora. From time to time Karen and I made the trip and sought to stimulate her memory by leafing through the old photo albums we left in her spacious room.

We had arranged for a private Seder meal the year after my father died, but the following year she suffered a stroke that left her virtually speechless. Tammy and I became orphans when Ima died on May 15, 2012. Both of us were relieved because her blank gaze had signaled she wished to break out of her internal prison.

Our mother was put to rest at the Children Of Israel Cemetery, alongside her husband of nearly sixty-six years.

Endnotes

1 "Is Anyone German Here? A Journey into Silesia," *The New York Times*, April 15,1990.

2 P. Chmiel, *Ostschlesien um die Jahrhundertwende in Spiegel der Volkzählungen*, "*Oberschlesisches Jahrbuch*" 6, 1990, pp 101–121.

3 J.J. Proszyk, *The History of the Jews in Bielsko (Bielitz) and Biala between the 17th Century and 1939.* Jagiellonian University, Kraków, Poland (2012).

4 *Juden in Südthüringen geschützt un gejagt, Band 6,* 1999, Verlag Buchhaus (Suhl).

5 *A History of the Weil-Sandler Family: From Prosperity in Germany to New Beginnings in the U.S.* Kindle Edition, 2016.

6 *Licht und Schatten-Ilmenau und St. Jakobus-ein Stück Zeitgeschichte,* Rainer Borsdorf, 2013.

7 'More than 1,000 died' trying to flee East Germany. *The Daily Telegraph*, August 13, 2003, citing a report by The August 13 Society.

8 "Encounters with Anti-Semitism," Part 5 of a Leo Baeck Institute online exhibit.

9 *Juden in Südthüringen*, Vol. 6, pp.205-6 Verlag Buchhaus Suhl, 1999.

10 *Ibid.* p. 214.

11 *Jüdische Nachbarn in Ilmenau*, Borsdorf et. al., 2018, Gegen Vergessen—Für Demokratie, Berlin.

12 British White Paper of June 1922, The Avalon Project, Yale University.

13 United States Holocaust Museum.

[14] *Ibid.*

[15] *Life in the Third Reich*, Richard Bessel, ed., 1987 Oxford University Press.

[16] *The Arab Community During the Mandate*, U.S. Library of Congress Country Studies.

[17] *Quellen zum antisemitischen Pogrom in Thüringen 1938.* Harry Stein, Zeitschrift für Geschichtswissenschaft, #10, 1988, VEB Deutscher Verlag der Wissenschaften, p. 900.

[18] *Ibid.,* p. 901.

[19] StA Weimar, *Generalstaatsanwalt beim Oberlandesgericht* Jena, Nr. 438 p.159.

[20] Stein, *op. cit.,* p. 906.

[21] *Four Thousand Lives: The Rescue of German Jewish Men to Britain, 1939* Clare Ungerson, The History Press 2014.

22 *Yad Vashem.*

[23] *Who's Who in Nazi Germany.* Robert S. Wistrich , Routledge, 1995, pp. 218–219.

[24] *Thüringisches Hauptstaatsarchiv.*

[25] *I Will Plant You A Lilac Tree.* Laura Hillman. Atheneum, 2005.

[26] Etzel website (*etzel.org.il*).

[27] Jewish Virtual Library, citing Knesset data.

[28] ”*The Man Who Opened the Wall,*” Michael Meyer, *The New York Times,* November 6, 2015.

Barbara Balkin

About the Author

Sam A. Gronner began his professional writing career as a journalist even before his 1970 graduation from the City College of New York. His byline has appeared in *The Record*, serving northern New Jersey, after stints at the now-defunct dailies *Newark Evening News* and *Elizabeth Journal*. He then spent a decade as a writer and editor in the national office of the Anti-Defamation League.

Gronner joined the public relations department of AT&T in 1984. He followed the spinoff of the company's equipment business into Lucent Technologies in 1996, eventually capping his corporate career as lead spokesperson for its wireless communications business.

In July 2001 he accepted an incentive to leave Lucent and immediately formed an independent public relations and corporate communications consultancy, primarily serving technology clients. He continues to offer writing services on a freelance basis.

A New Jersey resident, Gronner is married to the former Karen Widder. Between their two bicoastal children, each married, they have three grandchildren.

CPSIA information can be obtained
at www.ICGtesting.com
Printed in the USA
BVHW081506090522
636461BV00004B/23